Managing Part-time Study

Managing
Part-time Study

A Guide for Undergraduates and Postgraduates

Caroline Gatrell

Mc Graw Hill

Open University Press

Open University Press
McGraw-Hill Education
McGraw-Hill House
Shoppenhangers Road
Maidenhead
Berkshire
England
SL6 2QL

email: enquiries@openup.co.uk
world wide web: www.openup.co.uk

and Two Penn Plaza, New York, NY 10121-2289, USA

First published 2006

A catalogue record of this book is available from the British Library

ISBN-10: 0 335 21939 X (pb)   0 335 21940 3 (hb)
ISBN-13: 978 0 335 21939 1 (pb)   978 0 335 21940 7 (hb)

Library of Congress Cataloging-in-Publication Data
CIP data applied for

Typeset by RefineCatch Limited, Bungay, Suffolk
Printed in Poland by OZ Graf. S.A.
www.polskabook.pl

The *McGraw·Hill* Companies

This book is dedicated to

Tony
and
Anna and Emma
and my parents Pam and Max

Contents

Acknowledgements   ix

Introduction   1

1   To be or not to be a part-time student? Choosing and starting your course, and planning ahead   6

2   Getting down to it – strategies for managing your own learning   34

3   Practical tips for writing assignments, dissertations and theses   72

4   Plagiarism, referencing and originality   96

5   Coping with exams   109

6   The mid-term blues: getting stuck, and staying on course   117

7   What next?   150

References   156

Index   159

Acknowledgements

Had I not been a part-time student, this book would never have been written. My original (full-time) qualifications were in History of Art. However, my present career as a writer and an academic has developed as a consequence of gaining, from Lancaster University (where I now teach), an MBA and a PhD, both on a part-time basis. So the thanks below are due not only to those who have been with me through the process of writing this book, but also those who supported me during my previous years of part-time study.

First and foremost I would like to thank Tony and my parents Pam and Max for all their support while I undertook my MBA and my PhD. A very special thanks is owed to Tony, who lived through the PhD experience and was encouraging throughout. And thanks are due to my parents, both of whom, among other things, drove me quite long distances to research interviews when I was expecting Anna and Emma respectively.

I would like to thank those who offered academic guidance during my part-time study days – to David Brown, who supervised me during some major life changes – a wedding, an MBA, two babies and a PhD. Also to Rosemary Deem, for her wise counsel and for her continued support.

Thanks are due to many of my colleagues from past years – David Allen and Sue Brimelow who first sparked off my interest in Management Studies, and Richard Crail who encouraged me to embark on my MBA.

In my present role, I would like to thank my friends and colleagues who have supported me both in my role at Lancaster and in the writing of this book, especially John Mackness and Sally Watson. A very special thank you to Sarah Baines and Sarah Patterson (and thank you, Sarah P., for reading and commenting on drafts).

A debt is owed to my good friend Tony Watson for his ongoing mentorship and support in terms of both my own writing, and in relation more generally to the issues associated with part-time degree programmes.

Thanks go to all at Open University Press whose input to this book has been invaluable, and also to the reviewers for their helpful comments on the proposal which have helped to shape the book.

I would like to thank Rowena Murray for her friendship and for sharing her knowledge of writing practices which has been of personal benefit to me. Also thank you to those who took part in the 2005 Scottish Writers' Retreat, which definitely spurred me on through the mid-term blues when I was halfway through the book!

Of course, a big thank you is owed to all those who contributed to the book with student experiences, which I am sure will enable readers to feel that they are not alone – someone else really knows what it feels like to be a part-time student.

Finally I would like to say a very special thank you to my friends in the PhD pressure group (in particular to Sharon for her input at the start of this project). So a very big thanks to all those who shared the trials and tribulations of part-time PhD study with me, namely: Sue Eccles, Carole Elliott, Sarah Gregory, Ellie Hamilton, Valerie Stead, Elaine Swan, Sharon Turnbull and Helen Woodruffe-Burton.

Introduction

Undergraduate and postgraduate degrees – differences and similarities for part-time students • Challenges in common – the problems faced by all part-time students • The aim and structure of this book – and what is not included

Part-time academic study is a major life decision. It involves considerable investment both in financial and in personal terms, and the journey towards completion can be long and demanding.

Managing Part-time Study: A Guide for Undergraduates and Postgraduates is aimed at the growing number of students who are undertaking academic courses part-time, sometimes after a lengthy break from education. Unlike full-time students, many part-timers are already juggling full-time jobs with other interests and responsibilities. Some may be early career graduates getting to grips with new roles as managers or professionals at the same time as coping with a first mortgage. Other part-time students will be contributing to general household income and might have practical responsibilities towards children or elderly parents. Some readers may have left the education system once they had finished school, this being their first experience of higher education. Many of you will have jobs requiring long hours and/or travel and part-time academic study will impact not only on your own lives, but on employers, partners and dependants. All readers might be involved in sporting or social activities, which often drop to the bottom of the priority list when part-time study is involved.

Although there are many and varied study guides presently on the market (some of which might include a short section on doing a degree part-time), few of these focus on the challenges faced by part-time students.

The purpose of this book is to offer the kind of advice and encouragement that part-time students find it difficult to source elsewhere. *Managing Part-time Study* recognizes that the issues confronting part-time students are sometimes quite different from those faced by full-time students. This book identifies the particular pressures facing part-time students, and outlines the practical steps that might be taken to manage these challenges. For example, it provides guidance in dealing with the problems caused by combining study with other commitments (usually jobs and family) over a prolonged period; managing part-time relationships with faculty and other students; coping with exams; what to do when things have gone wrong and beating 'writer's block'. If you are a part-time student, you can counteract some of these challenges by developing strategies to suit you and your lifestyle, which will enable you to keep going and to succeed.

Managing Part-time Study brings together a wide range of ideas and research that will be helpful for part-time students. It draws upon my own experience both of teaching part-time students, and of being a part-time student myself for over ten years. It also features advice and know-how from other part-time students – some of whom have finished their programmes, some of whom are still living through the highs and lows of part-time study.

In response to the issues faced by part-time students this book offers strategies which will help you, throughout the study process, to:

- decide which method of part-time study is right for you;
- manage your own learning;
- sustain your motivation;
- prioritize the demands on your time;
- manage the practicalities of writing, whether for assignments or producing a dissertation or a thesis;
- cope with exams;
- anticipate and plan the challenges which you will encounter;
- deal with the difficult times (including feeling demotivated and getting behind with your work);
- decide what to do when your degree course has finished;
- understand how other students have lived through the experience of part-time study.

Undergraduate and postgraduate degrees – differences and similarities for part-time students

It is acknowledged that readers of this book will be working at different levels within the academic system, and will be studying across a wide range of academic disciplines. However, this book is constructed on the principle that, no matter what the academic level or subject matter, all readers will share issues in common (such as time management and isolation) because they are learning on a part-time basis.

Some readers may be embarking on the foundation course for their first undergraduate degree; other readers will be undertaking research for their PhD. It is recognized that the intellectual demands of postgraduate, or 'higher', degrees will be different from the demands of undergraduate degrees. Undergraduate readers of this text will be learning, in the main, about other people's ideas. You will be learning how to critique the work of others, and how to make the connections that will provide a good grounding in a given subject. If you are an undergraduate, you will probably be given a prescribed reading list, and choices about what you write will be limited because of the academic requirement to cover 'basic' and important areas of knowledge within your field. However, you may be required to understand things from more than one perspective and you will probably be required to produce a dissertation at the end of your programme, an exercise demanding initiative and the ability to study independently. While it is difficult to quantify how much you will have to write (as each course will have its own specification) it is probable that undergraduate assignments will be around 2–3000 words long and an under-graduate dissertation 10–12,000 words long.

Masters degrees and other postgraduate courses may be less directive, and if you are studying at this level, you will be expected to read above and beyond the recommended texts, and to produce a dissertation which shows that you have done some original research (especially if you are doing an MPhil or an MLitt). Masters students might typically be expected to produce assignments of 3–5000 words and dissertations might vary from 15,000 words in length to as many as 50,000 words, if the Masters degree is at MPhil or MLitt level.

If you are a PhD student, you will be expected to develop your own ideas, building on the academic work of others. PhD students are required to produce work which makes an 'original contribution' to their field of knowledge. If you are working towards a PhD you will need to acquire an excellent knowledge of the literature not only in your own field, but in associated areas. Your thesis will be a weighty tome – probably 70–100,000 words in length.

Challenges in common – the problems faced by all part-time students

It is thus recognized at the outset that the academic level at which readers of this book may be studying might vary. Nevertheless, the difficulties faced by part-time students are similar, whether at undergraduate or postgraduate level. The length of time required to sustain motivation when studying on a part-time basis may be prolonged. An Open University UK undergraduate degree will typically take six years to complete. Students working towards a part-time masters degree (e.g. MA, MSc, MEd or MPhil/MLitt) might expect to study for between two and five years. And part-time PhD students will take on average six to seven years to produce and submit a thesis. During these lengthy periods, all part-time students, regardless of the intellectual level at which they are working, will have to manage course commitments (which may include paying hefty fees) alongside changing life circumstances. Sustaining academic motivation for between two and seven years, especially when study is combined with other obligations, can be very hard. Students may feel isolated and lonely both intellectually and personally, because their day-to-day contacts with family and colleagues are probably unconnected with their academic work. Family, friends and employers will *expect* full-time students to place their degree high on the list of priorities. However, part-time students may have to fight to prioritize their academic commitments, possibly at the expense of relationships both at work and at home. Given these circumstances, the likelihood that some part-time students will fall behind with their work is much higher than for full-timers, as is the possibility that they may be obliged to take a break in study at some point during their degree. This is acknowledged and addressed in Chapter 6.

The aim and structure of this book – and what is not included

If you are a part-time student, the purpose of this book is to offer you the kind of understanding and encouragement that can be difficult to find elsewhere. By providing a map of the academic landscape, this book aims to equip you with the necessary tools to manage your own learning, sustain your motivation and anticipate the challenges which will be encountered. Much of the advice offered is relevant regardless of the intellectual level at which you are working. Where advice is specific to a particular academic level of study (undergraduate, postgraduate or PhD), this will be made clear. The feeling of walking into an exam room is much the same whether you are an undergraduate or a masters student. However, where the ideas may be different depending on the nature of your degree, this is made explicit and each case is dealt with in turn.

Managing Part-time Study is designed as a text that can be read all the way through at a single sitting or may be 'dipped into' when advice is sought on a specific topic. It aims to be non-prescriptive, but to assist you in finding the most appropriate solutions for your own situation, thus enabling you to 'stay the course'. The book is based on the following beliefs:

- Success at degree level depends on part-time students' abilities to take the initiative and manage their own learning.

- Part-time students are often 'cut off' from the mainstream activities within their institution. They need to work at developing student networks and keeping in touch with their university, thus ensuring that they are privy to important information and opportunities.
- A part-time degree is a personal journey, which cannot be reduced to a linear process, and no two students' experience is entirely alike. However, there are some general guidelines which part-time students can adapt to suit their individual circumstances and which will help them avoid/get through the difficult times.
- Every part-time student will have a different set of study/work/life challenges to balance, and will need to find their own way to prioritize the demands on their time.
- Sustaining motivation in these circumstances can be difficult and needs to be approached strategically.

What is not included

This book is designed to complement, but not to duplicate, texts which deal with the specifics of your degree programme (e.g. Phillips and Pugh 2005), and the focus throughout is on the particular challenges faced by part-time students, many of which are not covered in detail in other books. General advice with reference to part-time study is therefore offered on assignment and dissertation writing, sitting exams and so on. If you are seeking in-depth guidance, there are many good study skills guides available catering for a wide range of needs, some of which are referenced at the end of this book. This book does not attempt to replace specialist texts, or those which consider a single aspect of study in depth such as those aimed at helping you pass exams (Tracy 2006), write a thesis (Murray 2002) or do well in specific academic fields (Flowerdew and Martin 2005). What this book does offer, however, is an understanding of the *additional* and particular problems associated with each of these issues *when you are a part-time student*.

It is important to remember that this book offers general advice on part-time study, but *this is not a substitute for understanding and following the guidelines and regulations relating to your particular institution and course of study*. Your institution should offer a student handbook or website explaining the rules, and it is important to read these and follow them closely throughout. For those undertaking a thesis, it is worth checking on the rules before you submit, as things may have changed in the years that have passed since you first registered.

Finally, it should be noted that all of the names and some of the details of those who have been kind enough to share their 'student experiences' have been changed, to protect the anonymity of individuals.

1

To be or not to be a part-time student? Choosing and starting your course, and planning ahead

The increasing trend for part-time study • Low completion rates of part-time degrees • Choosing the right course for you • Flexible options: flexible and distance learning • Advantages of learning at a distance • Disadvantages of learning at a distance • Before you begin your distance learning degree programme • Distance learning: summary of key points • Part-time 'presence' at university • Part-time 'present' study: summary of key points • Doing a PhD, or research degree, part-time • Doing a PhD part-time: summary of key points • Undergraduate and postgraduate part-time study: making your case for time and space before you start • Making your case for time and space in which to study: summary of key points • Studying part-time from overseas • Studying part-time from overseas: summary of key points • Financing part-time study • Financing part-time study: summary of key points

Part-time study has experienced a massive surge of interest over the last few years not only in the UK, but in Europe, North America and throughout the developing world. In a situation where a linear career has become rare and multiple employers are an expected part of organizational life, part-time qualifications can facilitate career improvement or change, or offer the chance to retrain following a period out of employment altogether. Some readers seeking promotion might undertake a part-time MBA to enhance their business and management skills; others who are tired of the 'rat race' might think of doing a history degree, perhaps with a view to becoming a teacher, or a creative writing degree, maybe in the hopes of following in the footsteps of J.K. Rowling.

The personal and career profile of a 'typical' part-time student shows that there *is* no 'typical' part-time student. You may be an employed, knowledge-seeking student, with an age range from 22 to 65 years (24 per cent of graduates go on to combine further study with employment). Alternatively, you may not be in paid work. You may be learning while parenting small children, while in between jobs or (increasingly commonly) once you have formally 'retired' from employment but are seeking new challenges and adventures. You might see your degree as directly connected to career progress, as in Jack's case, below, or you may be undertaking a part-time degree for the purposes of personal growth and/or career change. For example, the rise in doctoral study for non-vocational purposes has been dramatic. You may be taking your first steps towards an undergraduate degree, perhaps doing your first module with the Open University, or you may be part way through your PhD. Whatever stage you are at, and whatever subject you are studying, you are in good company, and part of an increasing trend towards part-time academic study.

Student experience

I started my MBA for two reasons, firstly because I was aware the bar was rising for employment (companies started to state 'MBA preferred'), but also because my work career was moving from a technical to managerial role and I wanted to know the area well.

(Jack, part-time postgraduate, MBA)

The increasing trend for part-time study

The Open University has around 200,000 students registered to study part-time from undergraduate through to PhD level and is the largest university in Europe. And in the UK alone, almost 300,000 students are registered at any time for part-time postgraduate study. Of the part-time postgraduate students registered with UK institutions, 94 per cent are currently domiciled in the UK with the remainder overseas.

With the growth in e-learning, the global and 'overseas' market also has the potential to grow rapidly, as students may register online and undertake a degree programme quite literally from home. Students can, therefore, become 'overseas' students without leaving their house because it is possible to register for online degree programmes across the world. The development of e-technology and networked learning now means that institutions offering part-time programmes can often offer these irrespective of the location of the potential student, provided that students have the funds for the fees and the ability to work online. Consequently a student in Singapore may choose to study in Canada or Australia, or a student from China, in the UK. The global market for part-time study is therefore large and growing, and an increasing number of students will need to address the challenges of combining academic commitments with those of home and work.

Low completion rates of part-time degrees

Despite the increase in the numbers of students registering for part-time degrees, however, completion rates are disappointingly low. This is because many part-time students find it an impossible challenge to combine study with other demands on their lives such as employment, or unpaid caring work. Part-time students find it difficult to maintain the energy, momentum and motivation required to reach the end of their programmes, especially when 'life gets in the way'. Many encounter obstacles which they had not foreseen, and feel ill-equipped to deal with these. Some will be studying at a distance from their educational institutions, attending only occasionally for modules (or perhaps never, if they are enrolled on distance-learning programmes). Others, having only just left university, will be struggling to combine study with first jobs. Giving up on part-time study is not uncommon, but it can be very disheartening, as it often means a loss of time and money, not to mention the feelings of discouragement experienced by those who perceive that they have 'failed', sometimes for the first time in their lives. For this reason, it is important to think through, before you begin, which is the right course for you. You will need to consider timescales, costs, and the relative advantages and disadvantages of distance learning versus part-time 'present' study.

Choosing the right course for you

You may already have chosen the course that you feel is right for you (in which case it is still worth reading through the various pros and cons associated with your chosen mode of study, since these might highlight some of the issues that you may face as you progress your studies). For those of you who are still unsure about what you intend to do, however, the variety of options available offers a wealth of choice, ranging from programmes with high levels of face-to-face contact between students and lecturers, and between the students themselves, to programmes which are based largely on online teaching and discussion. In making your decision about what to opt for, you need to consider not only your *academic* needs, but how important it is to you to have face-to-face or social contact, as part of your study programme. You will also need to think about the amount of time you have available to study on a day-to-day basis; the length of time you have available to complete your qualification (can you wait six years, or do you need it sooner?) and (last but not least) the amount of money you have available to finance your studies.

In the rest of this chapter, I will consider what is involved in both distance learning and part-time 'present' study at undergraduate and masters level, and I will outline the advantages and disadvantages of both. I will also talk about the highs and lows of studying for a PhD part-time. Some suggestions for getting prepared and counteracting the problems will be made, and I will build upon these in Chapter 2. The chapter concludes with a section on finance, and the importance of planning how you intend to fund your studies.

What if you have already chosen/begun your part-time course or research degree?

Even if you have already chosen your course (and perhaps already started it), this chapter will nevertheless be useful. Having an understanding of the likely benefits and problems associated with the various forms of part-time study can be useful at any stage of your programme, and will enable you to take advantage of the positive aspects of what you have chosen to do, as well as planning and being prepared for the pitfalls. It is never too late to do some financial planning, and a discussion about finances takes place at the end of this chapter.

Flexible options: flexible and distance learning

Some courses will offer a wide range of choice, with the chance to mix and match what you study within a range of options to match your interests and existing level of knowledge. Such study programmes usually describe themselves as offering 'distance' or 'open' learning. As Talbot (2003) explains, there is some confusion around these terms.

Flexible, or 'open' learning

Talbot describes 'open learning' as 'learner-centred', with 'an emphasis on learners having as much flexibility as possible over the time, place and pace at which they learn' (Talbot 2003:159). Talbot points out that, while the ideals of 'flexibility' espoused in the concept of 'open learning' might appear attractive in theory, in practice it may be difficult to undertake a degree where 'flexibility is, literally, "open ended" '. This is because

> although learners in higher education may have some flexibility over time, place and pace of learning, the degree of flexibility is not usually significant due to the administrative constraints of registration, semesterisation and assessment.

Talbot notes that the Open University defines

> ... open learning in a different way – meaning that you can register with the Open University at any stage in your academic career, regardless of whether you already hold formal qualifications.
>
> (Talbot 2003: 150)

Distance learning

More commonly, students wishing to organize study around other commitments will find themselves registering on programmes which are defined as 'distance learning'. Talbot defines distance learning as follows:

> Distance learning, as the word 'distance' implies, will usually take place remotely, usually at home or at work, although elements of it may take place on campus (for example study days or tutorials). It is characterised by two key elements:
>
> • Teacher and learner are separated but learning takes place under the auspices of an educational institution or organisation.
> • Learning materials and two way communication (rarely face-to-face) characterise the learning process.
>
> (Talbot 2003: 159)

Distance learning is one of the most popular forms of part-time study. In the UK, the Open University has around 200,000 students registered each year on both undergraduate and higher degree programmes (Open University 2004b). Open University students are supported by a course tutor/supervisor, and a student enquiry service. Increasingly, much of the work will be web-based and will take place online but some courses are still textbook-based at present. Many students have access to a computer conferencing system where they can share ideas and experiences, and an online library resource allows students to access journal articles, books, newspapers and other sources. At some point in their studies, many students attend residential schools where they meet tutors/supervisors and other students face-to-face. However, even this commitment can, in certain circumstances, be waived, with some students who are unable to attend in person being allowed to carry out an 'alternative learning experience' instead. Student assessment takes place mainly through assignments and examinations. Exams like these are usually organized in 'local' centres, meaning that travel distance is limited for most students. Joanna, a part-time Psychology undergraduate, describes her experiences below.

Student experience

All the Open University courses I have studied run from February to October, so you have a good break before you start again with Christmas and New Year off. Normal workload for the year is seven essays of experimental reports and a three-hour exam in October, and assessment is weighted 50 per cent for coursework and 50 per cent for the exam, so there's a lot riding on those three hours of scribbling.

To get an undergraduate honours degree with the Open University it takes six long years if you study a 60-point course each year. You can take more than one course but it would be very tough. In theory you can access face-to-face tutorial support, usually on a monthly basis. But I haven't taken full advantage of this facility because tutorials usually take place on a Saturday morning in (nearby town) or (large city some distance away) and clash with children's commitments. I do make a point of going to the exam revision day in September in (large city) – it's good for helping to get motivated to really get stuck into the revision.

(Joanna, part-time undergraduate, Psychology)

Although Open University is by no means the *only* university offering students the chance to study part-time and at a distance, it is the largest provider of this kind of study. I will therefore focus on the Open University and how it operates as an example of how part-time distance study works. To illustrate how students might progress through an Open University degree programme, I will describe the situation of students undertaking a 'distance learning' Open University BA (Hons) in Childhood and Youth Studies. The structure of this degree programme is similar to that of many other courses offered by Open University.

Assuming that Childhood and Youth Studies was your chosen area of interest, and depending on your existing qualifications, you would probably begin with a Level 1 course on 'An Introduction to the Social Sciences', or a general course on 'Understanding Health and Social Care'. If you were already working with children, you might opt for a combination of practice-based courses on 'Working with Children in an Early Years [or Pre-school] Setting'. Once you had completed your Level 1 work, you would be in a position to progress your degree, as well as having gained credit points to count towards it. The Childhood and Youth Studies degree programme on offer in 2005/06 was designed to be adapted by each student to suit her or his personal circum-stances and interests. Thus, if students were interested in working with chil-dren, but had never done so, or were already working with children and were seeking a practice-based degree, they could choose courses which best suited their own situation. For example, the 2005/06 course stated that it was 'designed for those who work or intend to work with children and young people, and for those who have more general interests in the new inter-disciplinary field of childhood and youth studies'. This degree programme offered the chance for students to

> ... develop a broad understanding of childhood and youth in its social and cultural context. The degree is structured to enable students to extend [their] knowledge and skills in a specialised area of study such as child development or it can have a more vocational leaning towards professional work with children.
>
> (Open University 2004b: 23)

Students choosing science- or arts-based courses with the Open University are offered the same approach. The kinds of degree programme on offer range widely, from Psychology, to Maths and Statistics, to Information and Com-munication Technologies, to Modern Language Studies or English Language and Literature.

An extended timeframe

An Open University undergraduate programme such as Childhood and Youth Studies provides the chance to work to a timeframe to suit your personal commitments and to gain a degree over several years. You can

> 'build' courses towards a qualification or you can take just a single course and not commit yourself any further at first ... you can mix and match courses from different subjects to build towards a degree ... courses are designed so you can fit studying around your work and other commit-ments – in fact about 80 per cent of our students are working while they study.
>
> (Open University 2004b:)

While studying with an institution such as this, each component of your qualification is 'worth' a number of points. You progress towards your degree by working your way through different 'levels' of increasing difficulty, starting with a short, 'openings' programme (worth 10 points) to prepare you for the challenge of working your way through increasingly higher levels of study (levels 1–3, usually worth between 30 and 60 points each). Gradually, in this way, you can work your way towards an undergraduate honours degree. You gain your qualification by completing the various courses offered as part of your degree programme, and adding up the points gained as you progress until you have gained a total of 360 points (120 of which must be at level 3). If you find that you have 'caught the bug' of part-time study, you can continue working your way up through the system, until you eventually gain a PhD.

Institutions offering distance learning packages should be well supported by experienced academic and administrative staff, so there will usually be someone whom you can contact if you are stuck. Some components of distance learning programmes may also be supported by large employers who will supplement the 'distance' element of the courses with regular meetings between students and tutors/supervisors, usually organized in the workplace.

Advantages of learning at a distance

There are many advantages to learning at a distance in the way described above. You do not have to be present at your institution except for occasional residential weeks (which may in any case be optional). This is ideal for those who are 'tied' to home and employment and would therefore find regular travel difficult, especially if this involved overnight stays. Distance learning may therefore be particularly attractive to those employed in jobs with limited flexibility, to single parents, and to students with disabilities or chronic illnesses.

Students with disabilities

Equalities legislation and policy should mean that all European institutions make reasonable adjustments to meet the personal requirements of students with disabilities or health needs. However, the design of university buildings and accommodation may sometimes mean that, in practice, part-time study involving 'presence' can be difficult for those with disabilities or health issues. Part-time present study might also involve you in securing the coordination of more than one agency – for example, if a student requires dialysis, this will require the commitment of health services and accommodation officers, as well as academic faculty.

Of course, if part-time present study offers the best academic option for you, it is worth pursuing, and hopefully your institution and the other agencies involved will facilitate your requirements. However, as Open University explains, they are well equipped and keen to encourage participation from disabled students, and their

> ... expertise in distance learning combined with a wide range of multi-media materials and personal support means [they] offer a much more accessible system than traditional means of study. If you're disabled, have a specific learning disability or medical condition, [OU] can adapt to meet your specific needs – in tutorials and exams and at residential schools [as well as] supplying many course materials in different formats.
>
> (Open University 2004b: 9)

The convenience of distance learning

For students who, for whatever reason, would find regular travel and 'presence' at university to be an added pressure on their already busy lives, distance learning offers a wonderful opportunity to access undergraduate and post-graduate study to suit their convenience. Thus, while students wishing to study management part-time can, for example, attend as part-time *'present'* students at many institutions (London Business School, Lancaster University Management School, Manchester Business School, the University of Central Lancashire, Cranfield University and Warwick University, to name but a few), it is equally possible to gain management qualifications through distance learning at Warwick University, Open University or Henley Management School.

The distance learning option also offers students the chance of registering at an overseas institution. You can, for example, gain an American MBA by registering with the University of Phoenix.

Greater flexibility associated with distance learning (including financial)

In addition, distance learning is usually more flexible than courses which require presence at university. This means that you can learn at your own pace and, if need be, over a longer period of time. If you are registered at under-graduate level with the Open University, you may find that there are few limits to the time you can take to complete your degree. So long as you keep going, you can gradually work towards building up your 'points' until you have reached degree level. This may make financial as well as academic sense. Year on year, distance learning is often less expensive than part-time present study (though the total fee may be high). If you are funding your own studies, there-fore, it may be easier to spread the costs over a longer period.

Although distance learning can sometimes feel lonely, many courses are well supported and, for students who are unable to attend residential events, there are usually opportunities for students to participate in online discussion groups, clubs and societies.

Finally, while all forms of part-time study require students to be well organized and self-disciplined, distance learning makes particular demands upon you to develop excellent skills in learning, personal organization and time management, which will remain with you long after you have completed your degree programme.

Disadvantages of learning at a distance

It is notable (but unsurprising) that the Open University brochure claims that, over the last thirty years, it has 'helped 2,000,000 people to learn' (Open University 2004a). This carefully worded sentence suggests that the interest in distance learning is high, and that many people seek to broaden their interests, or gain promotion, by undertaking part-time study. All that is demonstrated by the figure of 2,000,000, however, is a high number of good intentions on the part of Open University students. What the figure does *not* reveal is the number of people who have not yet succeeded (and who may never succeed) in gaining their part-time degrees over long periods of time via distance learning. For some students, the disadvantages of learning at a distance will outweigh the advantages, and you need to think carefully about what sort of person you are, and what you are seeking from your programme, before you choose this route.

Doing an undergraduate or post-graduate degree via distance learning may mean that, no matter how large or experienced your provider, there are times when you feel very isolated. You may feel unsupported by friends, family and work colleagues who have very different priorities from you, and who may even resent your part-time study. You might find it hard to find alternative sources of support from student colleagues whom you rarely see face-to-face. It is also easy to feel discouraged and unsure of yourself if you do not regularly meet face-to-face with your tutor/supervisor and lecturers. And if you disappear from an 'online' discussion group, it is less likely that this will be noticed than if you do not attend a regular, face-to-face class. Probably the most difficult aspect of distance learning is the requirement to remain motivated and to 'stick it out' over a lengthy period when you are not attending classes or learning sets on a regular basis. This can be exacerbated by the fact that you might not have 'signed up' for a full degree programme but may be working towards your desired qualification by building up credits, meaning that you can 'stop off' at any number of different exit points. While the method of gradually working your way through a degree programme without a specific commitment to reach the end can reduce the pressures of part-time study, it may also reduce your motivation ever to complete your course.

Joanna is an Open University student, studying for a degree in Psychology. Joanna began her studies four years ago and manages her degree programme alongside a full diary. She is employed four days a week as a manager within a university. She has three children, who were all primary school age and under when she started. Joanna provides a flavour of her experiences below.

Student experience

Choosing a course of study and how it works for me
I looked at two options, one of which meant being a part-time 'present' student at the university where I am employed, the other studying at a distance with the Open University. The option of studying part-time at my own institution would have meant attending lectures in work time. While I think they may have been prepared to be flexible about this, they would not have 'given' me the time, but would have expected me to 'pay back' the hours spent attending lectures. So that would have resulted in me having to stay longer at work to make up the hours I had missed.

When I embarked on my studies, getting home before school ended was important because Joe and Louise were at primary school and Jenny had a year to go before she started school. The Open University option was also much cheaper, although you might not think it, because part-time members of staff working at my university didn't get 'free' study even though we were studying in our own institution. The offer of fully subsidized fees only applied to full-time staff.

But I was entitled to apply annually for a bursary for an external course through staff development funds. This has worked well thus far and my employer has funded a high proportion of my studies. But I have worked things out so that, if one year they say 'no', I know that I can manage to keep going.

The great advantage of Open University study is that it can be done when and where you want. I can listen to CDs while I'm in the car coming to work and while I'm mopping the kitchen floor. I usually study for half an hour in the mornings, between 6.15 and 6.45 am, and then again after the children are in bed. Study at the weekends is generally very limited as there's just too many other things happening. But I take my books on holiday and study while I am by the pool. I love being able to do this, though the kids think I am mad.

You've got to be very motivated to study with the Open University, because it's a lonely road sometimes and partners and family can get pretty fed up with it at times. It's also addictive – I've been trawling the Open University website for a masters in Psychology and have already earmarked my next endeavour to start in May 2007 – but don't tell my husband!

(Joanna, part-time undergraduate, Psychology)

Before you begin your distance learning degree programme

It is worth thinking through all these points before you begin. It is also worth doing some serious planning before you sign up, so that you know, as far as possible, exactly what you are letting yourself in for.

Trying a 'taster' course at a distance

If you have never studied part-time before, or if you haven't engaged in any form of study at all other than at school, it is worth investigating whether you can try a 'taster' course before you begin the long haul. If the 'taster' route is possible, be honest with yourself about how enjoyable, and how practical you found this experience. Did you manage to submit all your work on time? Were you well organized, or did you find yourself under pressure, rushing your assignments and failing to get through all the course materials? Did you cope well with studying by yourself, or did you find it lonely and frustrating? And most of all, did you enjoy the content of what you were doing, or would you prefer to try something different? If you feel you managed your taster course effectively, and enjoyed it into the bargain, then the signs are good. If you found the experience difficult, stressful or dull, then think very hard before embarking on a degree programme at a distance.

Read the instructions carefully

If you are aiming to complete an undergraduate or postgraduate degree through distance learning, be sure that you have understood exactly what is involved and what it will cost (see the finance section on pages 29–33). While it may be possible to tailor your distance learning programme to suit your own needs, there will be some rules that you are required to follow. *Make sure that you are clear about these at the outset,* so that you end up with the correct range of topics and credits to enable you to graduate with the degree you hope to gain. This might sound obvious, but it is surprisingly easy to choose a route without much forethought and then be required to change direction, which might cost you time and/or money (see my own student experience below). For example, the Open University will award you an ordinary degree based upon the full range of courses (at the appropriate level) that they offer. Thus, if you are happy to acquire a degree without 'honours', you can pick and choose from a wide range of subjects, so long as you gain the correct number of credits at the right 'level'. However, if you seek to obtain an honours degree, you will need to choose a degree in a 'named' subject (such as the one discussed earlier in Childhood and Youth Studies). Your options will be limited to those which contribute to the learning in your chosen topic, and there may be some elements of your degree programme which are compulsory, so it is important that you read, and keep up to date with, the course requirements, choosing your options carefully at each stage and taking advice from university administrators if you are unsure.

Author's own student experience

In 1992 I was working for the British NHS. I was invited, at short notice, to do an Open University Certificate in Managing Health Services which was just under nine months in duration (including an examination). I'm not sure why I was asked to join the programme, but my place was paid for and it seemed like an opportunity, so I took it – especially because I had been told that I could build on what I had learned and eventually gain an MBA through the Open University. This seemed like a great idea. However, at the time I did not investigate further what doing an Open University MBA might involve, how much it might cost, or how far the Certificate in Managing Health Services would count towards a masters qualification. Nor did I ask whether my employer would be prepared to fund this.

In addition to the fact that most of the students were given a 'free' place on the Certificate in Managing Health Services, the NHS offered extra support by appointing two course tutors to organize the students into learning sets. The learning sets met once a fortnight and engaged in interesting discussion and case study work, facilitated by course tutors. The tutors gave verbal feedback on written work, offered advice about difficult concepts and provided classes on exam preparation. The course consisted of five assignments and an examination.

I really enjoyed doing the course. I found the content interesting and enjoyed the social, face-to-face contact with other students. We were a hard-working, competitive group who got on well together and organized many informal events based around our regular meetings. I discovered that working in this way was highly motivating and, although it meant giving up weekends and bank holidays to study, I handed all my work in on time and sailed through the course.

When it was finished, I enquired what else I needed to do to get the MBA. I was a bit surprised to learn that gaining an MBA in this way would require another five or six years' work. Furthermore, no one had told me (and I had never asked) about funding for further modules. Put simply, there wasn't any, and students were expected to pay their own fees from then on. Finally, I had not realized that only the Managing Health Services course was supported by on-site tutors and learning sets. Other modules took place entirely at a distance, with only one annual residential course to look forward to.

As a person who is 'sparked off' by face-to-face intellectual discussion, and who likes to make fairly quick progress, the thought of continuing part-time study for a further five to six years, mostly on my own, and with no funding, was nothing like as inviting as doing the sociable Managing Health Services Certificate had been. Instead of carrying on, I spent the next twelve months investigating part-time 'present' MBAs. I applied for, and gained, 75 per cent funding from the NHS to do a two-year, part-time residential MBA. I was also awarded a study bursary from my chosen university which, at that time, was trying to encourage public sector students. I had to cover part of the accommodation costs, and the cost of study materials, myself. It took me two years to obtain my MBA, which involved attending compulsory residential study weeks and working in learning sets with other students. The flexibility to choose different course options was limited, but for me this was offset by the opportunity to work face-to-face alongside other students, and see my course tutor regularly. The course was intellectually stretching but was also very social, which was an important part of the motivation for me.

I have no regrets about doing the Managing Health Services Course. I enjoyed it, and the learning it offered provided a good grounding for the intensive two-year MBA course. But it might have been more sensible, just before leaping into what was 'on offer', to have given more thought to what I sought to achieve in the end and what, for me, would be the best way of achieving it.

(Caroline, part-time postgraduate, MBA)

Distance learning: summary of key points

Advantages of distance learning

- You can be flexible about how you learn and can spread your learning (and costs) over an extended timeframe.
- You can 'stop off' and take a break when it suits you.
- Some face-to-face contact with faculty and other students may be on offer but this is not usually obligatory.
- Courses are usually well supported with online discussion groups and library facilities.

Disadvantages of distance learning

- You may feel very isolated.
- If you 'disappear' from online discussion groups this may not be noticed.
- You are less likely to experience 'peer pressure' to keep up with your studies than if you are studying with a group of part-time present students, all at the same stage on the course.
- The ability to 'stop off' and take a break from study might mean you never get started again.

Part-time 'presence' at university

Many institutions offer the chance to undertake undergraduate and/or post-graduate study as a part-time 'present' student. Part-time 'present' study might be interpreted in a variety of ways, and may range from evening or daytime attendance at university once a week, or once a fortnight, to residential week-ends or weeks. It is likely that the course curriculum and timetable will be clearly defined by the host institution, and will offer only limited flexibility in terms of what you choose to study, and how long you take to gain your degree. It is probable that the timeframe in which you are expected to complete your studies may be considerably shorter than if you are learning at a distance – for example, a masters degree will take you perhaps two years, as opposed to five or six.

The advantages of part-time presence

It is much easier at an early stage to feel 'part' of your university and of your course if your programme involves regular meetings with your tutor/super-visor and other students, especially if these are held in the university environment. If your course is structured so that all students register and complete at the same time, you will have the support of a peer group whom you will get to know well during the time you are working together. For some students (myself included), regular face-to-face contact with other students is important in terms of keeping a high level of motivation. Being honest about it, this way of studying can be a good deal more fun than distance learning, since social activities are usually mixed in with intellectual requirements. The social activities can themselves form part of the motiv-ation to study and keep going, since these enable you to position part-time study as 'social' and 'fun' as well as hard work. Although distance learning students can draw support from online discussion groups, it is (in my view) very hard to replicate the social experience of being part of a face-to-face group of students who are all doing the same thing, at the same pace, as yourself. Furthermore, for students who choose a course with a residential element, the ability to be away from paid work and from home for a period of time means that you can focus on study. Being away for up to a week can be hugely beneficial to study, and even regular afternoon or evening attend-ance guarantees you at least *some* ring-fenced time and space to prioritize your studies – alongside a group of people who are travelling in the same boat as you.

When you are in regular personal contact with your peers, you may find yourself in quite a competitive environment, which can be a positive force if you are struggling to keep motivated or meet deadlines. Additionally, while your student group or learning set may be competitive, your peers will also offer support by putting pressure on you to keep going when times are difficult. People are more likely to notice if you fail to attend a class in person than if you have disappeared from a web-board, and you will quickly have made good friends who want to keep you in the group, and will therefore be ready to offer support when you need it.

The disadvantages of part-time presence

There are, however, some undeniable disadvantages associated with being a part-time present student. Presence at your university places different demands on you than if you are learning at a distance. It might involve you in travel, and there may be quite substantial extra costs if you need to pay for accommodation. You might have to be away from work and family for extended periods, or at least for a day and/or evening every week or so. The attendance requirement of your course might make workplace travel difficult, and might seriously get in the way of your home life. Furthermore, institutions requiring you to be present are unlikely to be sympathetic if you are unable to attend particular sessions or modules. Classes and learning exercises are often arranged around those who are expected to be there and students who fail to appear (other than for reasons of ill-health or real personal crisis) may be regarded by both faculty and fellow students as inconsiderate and uncollegial – especially if non-attendance is a regular occurrence.

In addition, missed classes may be difficult, if not impossible, to 'make up' – especially if your course is based upon residential elements of more than a few days. Course modules will probably be spread over an academic year, and may not be repeated until the following year. Attending the residential parts of your course may be compulsory, and the degree may not be awarded without full attendance except in exceptional circumstances. Even if coursework has been submitted, students may be expected to gain a full attendance record before they can graduate. In the event of a course element being missed, it is not uncommon for students on degree programmes requiring 'presence' to be obliged to wait 12 months in order to do the module when it comes around again. In such cases, especially if places on the course are limited, the student who has missed a course element may be expected to pay extra, or even to drop a year and begin again.

There are, of course, financial and personal implications to the shorter timeframe usually involved in part-time present study, in that you will need more time available for course attendance and study, and the annual cost of your programme might be substantially higher than if you spread it over years.

Finally – although you are 'included' in the sense that you are part of a student group and can all enjoy progressing together at the same rate – some institutions are better at making part-time 'present' students feel part of university life than others. Averil Horseford, writing of her experiences over many years of being a part-time 'present' student, argues that:

Issues of exclusion remain prominent amongst part-timers. On the whole, many fail to become integrated within their university community, with all its benefits and frustrations. I attended many lectures outside of business hours and was sometimes required to use half-closed buildings which lacked canteen and library facilities – the normal services that full-time students take for granted. Not being taught in an adequate learning environment can easily lead to the feeling that you are a 'second-rate' student receiving a 'second-rate product'. Much of the part-time challenge lies within these factors and adapting accordingly.

(Horseford 2000: 13)

For other students, the part-time present element of their course, and the opportunity to make friends, socialize and share academic development with other students, surpasses the sense that they may be treated differently from full-time students. Imogen, undertaking a part-time course in political studies, has found the networks that she has made with others on the course to be invaluable, and an important part of her experience:

Student experience

I started studying in 2002 amidst considerable upheaval in my own life. The taught elements in my course exposed me to new ideas and perspectives and encouraged me to read and think again. The support from fellow students grew as we got to know one another and as we stayed on the university campus for a few days or a week at a time. The taught elements and essays took up the first two years of the programme with the dissertation in the last couple of years. And the fact that we were so sociable was immeasurably important in providing mutual support as I persevered through the assignments.

(Imogen, part-time postgraduate, Political Science)

Part-time 'present' study: summary of key points

The advantages of part-time 'present' study

- It is easier to feel 'part' of your university if your programme involves regular meetings with a tutor/supervisor and other students.
- If your course is structured so that all begin and complete at the same time you will have the support of a 'peer' group.
- Part-time present study can be sociable which is fun and motivating.
- Taking 'timeout' from work and home can be advantageous for your studies.

The disadvantages of part-time present study

- You may be involved in travel and accommodation costs.
- Attendance requirements might be problematic in relation to your job or your home life.
- It is hard to 'pick up' your studies if you get behind.
- Part-time 'present' courses may be expensive.
- Part-time 'present' students may feel left out of university activities in comparison with full-time students.

Doing a PhD, or research degree, part-time

The number of students wishing to study for a PhD or an MPhil in the subject of their choice has grown over the past ten years. Students choosing to undertake a PhD may do so for a variety of reasons – because they seek career enhancement or career change; because they wish to pursue an area of interest not directly related to their paid work or, increasingly, because they have retired from paid work and wish to follow the dream of undertaking an in-depth research project. Beginning a research degree (whether at MPhil or PhD level) is exciting but daunting, especially when you are combining study with paid work. It is not a course of action that should be undertaken lightly, because it will cost you dearly both in personal and financial terms. Bearing in mind that it takes on average three to four years to complete a PhD full-time, you will need to allow between four and seven (or even eight) years to obtain your PhD part-time. Beware of any advertising that suggests you may succeed in less time than this. It is arguable that institutions which offer part-time PhDs in four years or under are failing to acknowledge the average time it takes most students to complete. They are probably quoting only the *minimum* registration time (maximum registration limits are normally around eight or nine years), and most PhD students who do succeed in completing their PhD will take quite a bit longer than four years (more like six or seven) to achieve this.

Although it may also take you around six years to obtain an undergraduate degree, it is arguable that, for PhD students, sustaining motivation over the period of time required will be harder than for most other students in most other circumstances. This is because, even if your PhD contains a 'course' element, you will nevertheless be responsible for producing a substantial piece of original research, which can be a lonely and difficult challenge. Doing a major piece of research over a long period of time, when the only deadlines set are your own, can feel both socially and intellectually isolating even when you are a *full-time* student and resident at your university.

Doing a part-time PhD at a university near to you

For this reason, I suggest that part-time PhD students should think very carefully before embarking on a programme of study in which they are very distant from their institution. This is for a number of reasons. First, the ability to visit your institution, attend seminars and join student study groups will reduce the feelings of sometimes quite extreme academic isolation that may be experienced by part-time research students. Antonia Dodds, doing her part-time Social Science PhD, explains how low she sometimes feels due to her lack of a social and intellectual student network:

> I don't have an equivalent peer group to measure myself against [and] . . . the habitual complaint of academic isolationism is compounded by the fact that I know very few other part-time PhD students. Those who do study in the same mode as me are usually in a different situation, i.e. [some] already have academic jobs.
>
> (Dodds 2000: 57)

Of course, you can (and many part-time research students do) succeed in building up good support networks online. However, if you are studying within a reasonable travel distance of your institution, you may more easily mix online discussion with face-to-face contact. Visits to your institution may enable you to make informal connections with other students, and there may be reading or study groups which you can only discover by spending some time at your institution.

Another reason why undertaking your PhD in a location close to you is advantageous is because accessibility to the many small and informal seminars that take place every day within an active and intellectually exciting environment can provide an easy way of keeping you up-to-date. This is important, and is more of an issue for research students than for those on taught undergraduate or masters programmes. This is because while you may be responsible for your own learning on a 'taught' programme, course tutors/supervisors and convenors should *share* the responsibility for *directing* your studies, and for keeping you up-to-date. For PhD students, the expectation is rather different. You may have a tutor/supervisor to whom your area is 'of interest' but as you progress your studies, it is anticipated that *you* will become the 'expert'. Thus, while you may expect guidance from your tutor/supervisor, she or he may well rely on you to keep up-to-date and be aware of changing thought and developments in your field. You might also be given the chance to present your own work to student colleagues and other academics, which will provide you with an invaluable opportunity to gain academic feedback on your work, as well as the chance to gain confidence about presenting your thesis in public (which is rather different from the experience of doing work-related presentations). Online support cannot substitute for personal presence at informal or small events, as not all institutions are 'geared up' to broadcasting or posting things live on the web. Thus, the ability to 'drop in' to your university and join other students and academics in discussion at no extra cost can be invaluable, and might save you time in the long run.

Doing PhD research at a distance from your institution

It may be that you have no option other than to study at a distance from your institution, perhaps because you are researching a subject which is not available at a university near you, or because you wish to be supervised by a particular individual. If this is the case, you will need to be proactive about joining online discussion groups (though be careful to protect your intellectual property – see pages 102–3). You may find that, even if your own university is located some distance away, you can make arrangements to attend events at an institution which is closer to you, as a result of which you may be able to access some student networks or face-to-face study groups. This approach is working well for Jason, an international, or overseas, student who is registered at a UK university, and who has continued his studies from locations across the world.

Student experience

Combining an international career with being both a part-time and an international student is not easy, but it can be done. During my study, I have worked and lived in Yemen, Dubai and Australia which obviously resulted in many interruptions and possible 'excuses' for me not to continue my studies. Some subsequent tips that I would offer prospective part-time international students are: select a study area that truly interests you and that you can be passionate about; communicate back with your supervisors and fellow students on a regular basis; manage a realistic timing and review plan; and select relevant people back at home (perhaps from local universities or at work) whose views you value, and whom you can discuss your studies with. Basically, try to create your own local network as the regular face-to-face interaction with such people is important for you not to feel isolated or alone.

(Jason, part-time masters, and subsequently PhD, Management)

Whatever your situation, it is important to think through carefully whether you have the time, the patience and the money required to gain a PhD – and whether you can rely on support from family and/or employers over what will be a lengthy and sometimes stressful period of time. Successful completion of a PhD, and the possibility of using the title 'Doctor', is a great achievement and a real confidence booster. However, nobody who has gained a PhD part-time will underestimate the likelihood that, at times, you will feel lonely, demotivated and seriously fed-up. These factors may well account for the low completion rates of those who undertake part-time PhD study – in the UK, only around 30 per cent of students who begin a PhD part-time will ever complete it and, of that group, most will take between six and seven years in total.

Doing a PhD part-time *is* possible (I know, because this is how I did mine) but you need to think even more carefully than undergraduate or masters students about how you are going to manage part-time PhD study.

Doing a PhD part-time: summary of key points

- Try and register close to home so that you can maintain at least some presence at your university.
- Try to mix online discussion with face-to-face contact.
- Join reading or study groups where possible to minimize the sense of isolation that doing research part-time can bring.
- Attend seminars and other events as often as possible.
- Where possible take the opportunity to present your own work, verbally, to others present.
- Think through the difficulties of managing part-time PhD study before you begin.

Undergraduate and postgraduate part-time study: making your case for time and space before you start

The practical difficulties of combining part-time study with other commitments are discussed further in Chapter 2. It is possible that some of these problems might be avoided if you think about them before you begin. For example, when do you plan to study? If you have caring responsibilities, will these be affected? For those with older relatives or with children, might your need to study mean that someone else will be expected to take on more duties, or to manage with your doing less than you do at the moment? Joanna, who outlined earlier what it felt like to be a distance learning student with the Open University, was very conscious of the impact her study had on her family. Joanna takes a good deal of trouble to minimize this, managing without face-to-face tutorials and keeping weekends clear of study commitments. Nevertheless, Joanna was aware that her partner 'tolerated' her studies, and noted that, just occasionally, he 'throws a wobbly'. If you do need to consider the needs and wishes of family and friends, it might be worth a discussion at the outset, so that you can come to some sort of agreement (or at least set some boundaries!) before you start. See also the section on making yourself the priority on page 49.

Chrissie's example below shows that this can work and you can claim some regular time to study, even though this may not be easy.

Student experience

I am on my own with two teenagers and it is sometimes very hard. I am doing a part-time course in health and social care which my employers pay for part of. Which if I keep going, I can probably make it to a degree. My kids do nothing round the house and would never do any schoolwork without a row. So at the beginning I could not see how I could get through all this coursework.

So I said this to my manager and she said (to my surprise) that I could have her office and her computer every Tuesday morning to work on my course stuff. She goes to this other meeting and doesn't get in till lunchtime. Then I said to the kids, 'you are not babies any more', and I pushed both of them to get themselves to do their own breakfast and go to football on the bus on Saturday mornings (without me driving them), which they now do. Also I said 'no more ironing', and they have also agreed to iron their own things which they now do. And one of them in particular doesn't like to look scruffy, so I have stuck to what I said and if they don't iron things themselves then they go out creased.

Also, they have been better at doing school work than before because if I am sitting working, then sometimes they will sit down with me and get on with their own. So although it's been a bit of a battle, I think it is working well for all of us.

(Chrissie, part-time undergraduate, Health and Social Care)

Making your case for time and space in which to study: summary of key points

- Be aware that others will be affected by your study commitments.
- Negotiate boundaries with employers and relatives at the outset.

Studying part-time from overseas

If you are studying in a country which is overseas, you might face particular problems that are not a worry for 'home' students. In the next chapter, I include a section on part-time overseas study for those who are already registered, but there are some issues which you could consider if you have not yet begun your course. Mostly, these involve practicalities. Whether you are a part-time 'present' student or a distance learning student it is worth thinking through both the financial and personal costs of studying overseas and possibly in a different cultural context. For distance learning students, this might mean less face-to-face contact than others on your course. Even though others may be reliant mainly on e-mail contact, they may have access to regional tutorial meetings, and there may be informal student study meetings to which you are unable to go. For part-time present students, the costs, in terms of time and travel, may be very expensive and it is important to be sure exactly what the course requirement is before you start. For instance, do you have to attend for taught modules only, or will your student group be expected to meet in between modules to undertake projects or progress their assignments? And how much will it matter if you can't get to these meetings?

Even more than for 'home' students, it is worth doing a 'taster' course before you begin if at all possible. Distance learning students with the Open University can, for example, begin with an 'openings' course, in which some reading and written work is done with the support of a tutor/supervisor, but which is short and not too expensive. Maureen Moss, describing her 'openings' course, before embarking on her degree programme, recalls it as

> an ideal solution as it was only a three-month commitment and was reasonably priced; it gave me the opportunity to try distance learning and see if I could fit any learning into my lifestyle.
>
> (Maureen Moss, Open University)

If you wish to be a part-time 'present' student, it may be possible to try a one- or two-week summer school at your chosen institution. This will give you a realistic sense of how manageable the travel is, both in terms of time and expense. Having spent a week in the institution you have chosen, you will have a much clearer sense of whether the effort and expense required on your part to study as a part-time present student overseas is worthwhile.

Studying part-time from overseas: summary of key points

- Investigate whether other students may be able to access 'local' support which will not be available to you.
- Make sure you are clear about if, and when, you are expected to attend course elements in person.
- Try taking a taster course, or attending a summer school before you sign up.

Financing part-time study

Before I conclude this chapter on the various types of part-time study available, and how to make the best of what is on offer, I shall deal with the issue of financing part-time study. I have already noted that keeping up the motivation to continue part-time study can be difficult over a long period of time. I have not, however (other than in the example of my own experience, in which I found that my assumptions about funding were over optimistic), considered the importance of doing some serious financial planning before you begin. Doing a part-time course is a bit like going on holiday. When planning to go on holiday, you are advised to reduce the amount of clothes you plan to take by half, but double the amount of money you think you need. With part-time study, you need to think carefully about reducing your existing social and other commitments by half ... but allowing for substantially more money than the minimum. In the next chapter, I will talk about managing your time around part-time study. However, the discussion about finance needs to happen, if possible, before you begin (if you have already started your course it is never too late to think about your funding for the remainder of your study).

Why is funding an issue?

Many part-time students are self-funding, or are receiving financial support for study from employers. When they begin their programme, most part-time students are reasonably confident that they will be able to finance their study all the way through. Some, however, will face a shortfall at some point in their programme and this is usually for the following four reasons, each of which can be anticipated and, to some extent at least, addressed before they become a real problem. The four main reasons for lack of funds for part-time study are:

- Students are paying more than they need to.
- Students have underestimated the full costs of their programme.
- Students take much longer to complete their degree than they had planned.
- Students' financial circumstances have changed.

I will deal with each of these issues in turn and consider what might be done to prevent/alleviate problems.

Students are paying more than they need to

Many part-time students are self-funding, or are funded by their employers. In some instances, the student and/or the employee may be entitled to a reduction in fees, or may be eligible for a bursary. Such opportunities to pay a reduced fee are not always advertised by institutions, who may not themselves be aware of your circumstances. For example, some institutions may offer financial support to students who work in the public sector. Others may offer, or may know about the availability of studentships, or regional development monies. Some organizations such as the Open University encourage those student groups they particularly wish to attract, such as disabled students, to offset study costs with specially tailored grants and/or allowances. Before you begin your course, it is really worth doing some research. Start by reading the small print in university prospectuses and websites, just to see if you can spot an opportunity. Or ask the university administrator with whom you are dealing if they can offer any advice. You never know – it could just save you hundreds of pounds!

Students have underestimated the full costs of their programme

It is worthwhile sitting down and producing a draft budget for your programme. Even if you are hoping to claim some, or all, of your costs from your employer, it is helpful if you know in advance what these are. Many students find that 'hidden' or unanticipated costs take them by surprise. For example, it is important that you have really understood the fee structure of your course. Will the fee you are paying remain constant during the time you are registered, or will it increase each year – and if so, by how much? What happens if you suspend your studies for a time, or fall behind and require extra time to complete your course? Will you still be liable for a full fee over the full academic year?

Furthermore, what equipment might you be expected to buy? Full-time students can probably assume that technological equipment will be available on campus, even if this has to be shared. Part-timers, on the other hand, might find that they are denied access to faculty laboratories or workstations (perhaps for the simple reason that part-time sessions take place after hours and the labs are closed). As a part-timer, you may be expected to buy, or hire, expensive equipment or computer packages, especially if your course is in a science subject. It is worth checking out in advance what is available to you, and what is regarded as your own responsibility. Part-time distance learners might be able to borrow what they need from their institution – but should enquire in advance whether this is a 'right' or a privilege. Can you automatically assume that equipment will be on loan to you or will it depend upon how many other students seek to borrow equipment/software? And will it be free, or will you be charged a hire fee?

Distance learning students may be able to attend summer schools or 'crammer' courses. Check in advance whether the cost of these is included in your course fee, or whether you are expected to pay for part, or all, of your stay.

If you are a part-time 'present' student, you may incur heavy transport and accommodation costs during your course. Try and be realistic about these. If you live some distance away from your institution, is it feasible to think that you will travel there and back in a day? Or might you find, on occasions when everyone is working late, that you are just too tired and you need to pay for an overnight stay? Can you be guaranteed a room in university accommodation (and is this really cheap, or might it be quite expensive)? Or is this only on offer during vacations, leaving you to fund hotel costs during term time? Will transport costs remain the same during the period you are doing your course, or is there a danger that they might creep up? This is particularly relevant if you are an overseas student on a part-time course which requires 'presence' as in Al's case below. It is worth thinking all this through at the outset and building in some some 'contingency' money in case things don't go to plan.

Additionally, although many journal and newspaper articles can be accessed online, have you allowed for the purchase of books? Your university library may be a good source of material when you are pursuing an individual project – but what if a whole group of students are working on the same topic? Will there be enough textbooks to go round, or will you need to buy your own copies?

Student experience

I registered on a course in the UK which involved three visits per year to my university. My employer was paying the fees but the travel was my problem. When I started, there was a budget airline offering fares at rock bottom.

But unfortunately, they went belly-up and then I was into some pretty expensive trips. This was my problem, as I said – but it was a pretty costly one, and not something I had really figured into my budget. I managed it – but it was tough on my partner who then had to take the lion's share of our holiday costs, because my budget was a bit stretched.

(Al, part-time postgraduate, Executive Management Programme)

If you are being funded by your employer or another body, it is worth checking what the policy is should your (or their) circumstances change. What if you change jobs, or decide to switch courses, or drop out of your academic programme altogether? Can your sponsors oblige you to refund the money they have spent on your behalf?

Finally, if you are being funded by your employer, or by a grant, make sure you get them to put their promises in writing. That way you will both be clear about what their commitment is – and if, later in the day, the organization changes its mind, you will have written evidence to back up your claim to entitlement to the payment of course fees. This will make it harder for them to withdraw their support, as in Janet's case below. If you think through cost-related issues such as these in advance, you may find that your overall costs look rather more intimidating than you had imagined. This might get things off to a depressing start – but at least you will know where you are, and you will be less likely to come in for any financial shocks.

Student experience

My organization said that it would be happy to fund my course. The course was, and is, central to my job role so this seemed reasonable on both sides. However, this agreement was verbal and they later changed their mind, by which time I was already well established on my course. I was horrified, as this was totally unexpected and very upsetting.

First of all, I had to find the money to pay for the course fees. This wasn't going to be easy as I had just taken on some other financial commitments and wasn't really in a position to manage something unanticipated. And secondly, I felt they had let me down. They are an organization which claimed to want to fund staff development but when it came down to it, for no good reason, they changed their tack and withdrew my funding. I suspect that this was because when I started my course, they expected to have some wealthy clients whom they wrongly imagined would fund the staff development.

But things didn't go quite the way they planned. And then my organization weren't prepared to 'take the hit' so they landed the course costs back on me, personally, without warning or proper explanation. I think in future I would always get a promise like this in writing. And I would ask them what contingencies there could be if the situation changed.

(Janet, part-time postgraduate, Information Technology)

Students take longer to complete their degree than they had intended

When planning out a timeframe for completing a degree, students often underestimate how long it will take them to complete it. This is more likely to be the case for distance learning students, and for research students, who can be more 'flexible' about how and when they do their work, than for students on more structured courses requiring part-time presence. The planning and writing of assignments, or writing up of research, often takes far longer in practice than it might appear at the start. For example, taking two distance learning modules a year at undergraduate or masters level might seem like a possibility before you start but – as Joanna observed earlier in this chapter – just doing one module is quite enough if you have other commitments to consider. And, as I have already mentioned, PhD study, while minimum registration times might be only four years, usually takes six to seven years.

Scott Holtham, taking a masters degree in literature with Open University, describes how the crafting of a 1500-word essay took him far longer than he had thought:

For an MA essay, particularly in literature, it just isn't possible to waffle your way to a high mark. There is no escaping the diligence required at this level of scholarship . . . my first essay took much longer than anticipated. It was only supposed to be 1500 words but it took me hours, days, to draft and redraft.

(Holtham 2000: 75)

What this means financially, of course, is that you need to plan for the 'worst case scenario'. What will it cost you if it takes you far longer than you imagined to complete each module, or finish your research degree? What if, instead of achieving your goals in the minimum registration period, you find that you require the *maximum* amount of time to complete your degree? Can you afford the fees and the 'on-costs' every year? And if you are sponsored by an employer or other funding body, are they willing to stay with you for the 'long haul', or are their funds and/or promises limited? Furthermore, have you talked through the financial implications of your study with 'significant others'? Will your continued payment of course fees impact, for example, on what you can afford to do holiday-wise? Although, of course, you can't plan for everything, you can think ahead, and allow for completing your course in the *maximum*, as opposed to the *minimum*, registration time.

Students' financial circumstances change

Some things are difficult to plan for. What if you or someone close to you is made redundant and money is tight? Or what if you become sick, and are unable to continue paid work? What if your firm changes its policy and ceases to fund staff development, as in Janet's case, above? If at all possible, it is worth building in a bit of 'rainy day' money at the start of your study. If there is any way you can afford this, one year's fees tucked away in a savings account – even if your employer appears set to fund your whole course – could prove a life-saver if things go wrong financially while you are studying, and might just make the difference between carrying on or giving up.

Financing part-time study: summary of key points

- Check whether you may be eligible for bursaries or reductions in course fees.
- Ensure you have worked out the full costs of your programme, including books, accommodation, IT requirements, travel costs and attendance at summer schools.
- If funded by your employer, check their policies – what happens if you leave, or they change their mind about paying fees? Where possible, get promises in writing.
- Plan financially for the maximum completion time.
- If you can afford this, put away some money for paying fees on a 'rainy day', in case your financial circumstances change.

2

Getting down to it – strategies for managing your own learning

I believe that the key to successful part-time distance study and research is to take responsibility for your own progress: nobody else can do it for you.
(Paul, part-time PhD student, Religious Studies)

Settling down to a part-time course • What to expect (and what not to expect!) from your university • Managing your own expectations: summary of key points • How to manage your own learning • Prioritizing yourself and your studies • Part-time study and home life • Strategies for managing your own learning: summary of key points • Part-time study and overseas students • Overseas, or international, students: summary of key points • Working in groups • Working in groups: summary of key points

The ability to manage your own learning is key to part-time postgraduate achievement. For part-time students, the ability to motivate yourself to prioritize your academic work, meet deadlines and position yourself as the driving force in the study process is essential. The purpose of Chapter 2 is to help provide the foundations for getting going, which will enable you to make good progress. Many part-time students find it difficult to get going, and keep going, to work independently and take responsibility for their own learning at the beginning of their programmes – often more so than they had anticipated. The first part of this chapter deals, therefore, with the reasons why part-time postgraduates find it difficult to settle down. It also underlines the importance of starting out with realistic expectations, both in relation to your institution and to yourself. An early understanding of what is on offer is important, because it can save a good deal of disappointment and wasted time later on. For students who want to do well, prioritization and self-managed learning are challenges which need to be confronted from the word 'go'. The second part of Chapter 2, therefore, offers practical advice about how to plan and manage your own learning. In this chapter, I explain:

- why settling into a part-time course may be difficult;
- what to expect (and what not to expect) from your university or college;
- how to motivate yourself and get going;
- how to plan and manage your own learning;
- how to prioritize yourself and your studies;
- the issues facing students studying part-time overseas;
- the challenges of group work;
- feeling 'different' because of your gender or ethnic background.

Settling down to a part-time course

Let's assume you have begun your programme of study. You have decided on your topic, gained your place at your chosen college or university, and perhaps even begun your coursework. You may be paying your own tuition fees, which could be quite an undertaking, especially if this is an expensive science or business-based degree programme. You may have met some of your fellow students, whether face-to-face or online. But you probably don't know any of them very well: you don't know how good, bad or indifferent their academic work will be and you don't know which of them will 'stay the course'. You are probably not entirely clear about what the expectations of your institution will be, or what standard of work they will expect. You are busy at work and at home, and may be unsure about where and how you are going to find the time you will need, in order to do the work required.

There are many books already on the market (including one written by me, with Turnbull, 2003), which offer good advice on study skills, time management and so on. There are also some first-class texts on how to write – the most helpful of these, in my view, is Rowena Murray's (2002) *How to Write a Thesis*. The principal focus of these books, however, is not the part-time student. So while I intend, here, to cover some best ways in which to get going, practical guidance will not be the only focus. In addition to providing 'handy tips', Chapter 2 will examine common problems from the very particular perspective of the part-time student and will explain why these obstacles can seem so difficult. This is because understanding the reasons *behind* learning challenges can be a big first step towards overcoming these, and making progress. Before I begin the discussion on 'getting started', therefore, I am going to make some suggestions about why part-time higher education can seem daunting – even to students who are senior managers, and/or to those who have been to university before.

What to expect (and what not to expect!) from your university

This [part-time] course is anticipated to become the next generation programme in education. The intention is to break the mould of [postgraduate] education.
(University prospectus, description of a part-time degree programme)

Unlike many programmes on offer . . . the aim of this innovative part-time programme is to provide a forum for debate, reflection and discussion.
(University prospectus, description of a part-time degree programme)

Both of the above anonymous quotes are taken from glossy brochures advertising part-time study at universities in the UK. One of the explanations for why part-time postgraduate students sometimes feel let down and disappointed when they begin their courses is because they had little idea of what to expect from their university at the outset. Universities are in competition with one another to attract good students. This can sometimes lead university advertising materials to be over-optimistic about the experience of part-time study by emphasizing the benefits, without necessarily going into detail about the problems, or the extent of work required to gain a degree part-time.

Courses aimed at the 'executive' market, in particular, are seeking students who are employed and may be climbing their way up the business, technology or public sector ladders. The promotional materials associated with such programmes may be particularly guilty of waxing lyrical about part-time study, often referring to students as 'participants', or even 'clients', while glossing over the academic requirements. Brochures and websites also tend to focus on seductive intangibles such as 'creating virtual intellectual spaces' as opposed to specifics such as 'the course tutor/supervisor will be available for real-time online discussion every Monday morning, 10–12 am, New Zealand time'.

Disappointment may also occur because students who have previously studied at university full-time (perhaps especially if they are mature students) think back to university and college life with a sense of nostalgia. It is easy to recall through rose-tinted spectacles the 'relaxed' atmosphere of undergraduate days when study was the priority and personal responsibilities were often less onerous than they may become later in life. Managing the requirements of part-time study while keeping the rest of your life (employment, your home, caring responsibilities and so on) ticking over is a very different scenario. Students beginning part-time study often experience a sharp 'low' just after they have started, which can be demotivating. Part of the key to taking charge of your own learning is in starting out with a realistic outlook in the first place about what will be on offer from your institution and what will be required from you as a part-time student.

Being used to coming first

To begin with, if you are a student who is in paid employment, you will have quickly become used to being part of an organization which makes you and your needs the main priority. Your employer probably spends substantial sums of money on setting up systems to enable you to get on with your work without interruption. This might sound questionable at first, and I realize that the image of the caring employer who makes your needs the priority might not immediately ring bells if you are rushed off your feet as a health professional or are a busy middle manager working within a huge corporation. But just think about it for a minute. In your workplace, you probably have access to a computer and an e-mail account which somebody else, somewhere else, has set up for you to use. You might have your own desk, or maybe even your own office, which will have been provided for you from the minute you arrived. If you or your profession has particular needs (for example, doctors or nurses in training) your organization or professional body will have gone to some trouble to accommodate these.

Unless you are self-employed, your employer will have established when and how you work, and will ensure that your pay and tax are properly calculated, and paid into your bank account on a given date each month. Your organization – even if it employs large numbers of people, and even if it does this purely for economic gain – will be 'individualistic' to the point that it will take quite a bit of trouble to tailor itself to your requirements and provide you with what you need to be able to do your job properly. In the same way, if you are not in paid work but at home full-time, you will have organized things to suit your own convenience, even if money is sometimes tight. Your own preferences and the individual needs of those with whom you live will be reflected throughout your household and your daily life.

Colleges and universities, on the other hand, are usually less focused on the requirements of individual students but are principally concerned with the general needs of the majority. They tend to be 'collective' institutions, providing more or less the same facilities for everyone. They are therefore unlikely to arrange things around you and will, instead, expect you to fit around *their* requirements and timetables. Most students will have to conform with what is on offer, even if it is not their preferred choice. For example, unless you can provide a very convincing argument that you are an exception to the rule (e.g.

you have a disability), your university is unlikely to reconfigure its IT systems, or invest in some new piece of technology, just for *you* – it would only do so for the benefit of everyone. Furthermore, dates for courses, exams and programme deadlines will be set well in advance and as a student, even if you are very senior in your field and even if you are registered on an expensive 'executive' programme, you will be expected to fit in with these. This is likely to be the case even if you are learning flexibly and at a distance. As Talbot (2003) points out, even institutions trying to be student-centred in their approach will be catering for large numbers and will be constrained by the requirements of registration, timetabling and assessment.

Finally, a good university will provide you with some support from a tutor/ supervisor, but this will be no more, and no less, than the assistance offered to others on your course. Furthermore, this support will be rationed. Tutors and supervisors – whether teaching on part-time 'present' or distance-learning programmes – will have workload allocations clearly set out well in advance. They will not be prepared to give more than a fair percentage of their time to one student. Thus, as a part-time student, you will find yourself one of many. And while this may be unproblematic to full-timers, who can more easily organize their lives around study and the requirements of the university, it can be quite difficult for part-timers, who are trying to tailor part-time study to fit around other things they are doing with their lives – especially if the university concerned has implied, through its advertising materials, that programmes might be more individualized than they actually are. (In contrast to this, however, it is worth noting that universities and colleges can be very helpful when it comes to dealing with genuine and exceptional personal issues – for example ill health or disability.)

Check out what is available

One key to avoiding disappointment and frustration (which can be very demotivating) is for you to be clear at the outset what practical support is on offer and what you can reasonably expect. By the time you begin reading this chapter you may well have chosen your university and begun your course of study. However, it is still not too late to read the small print. Look carefully through the details on your course website or student handbook. Figure out what you are entitled to, and what level of support has been promised. If you are still unsure, then contact your course adviser and ask what *existing* facilities you might be able to access to meet your requirements. Then work out how best you can use what is on offer, rather than trying to persuade your institution to change their ways to suit your needs. This might be particularly important for part-time 'present' 'executive' students, who may be persuaded that they are likely to receive specially tailored IT services, 24-hour on-call tutors/supervisors and so on ... only to discover that, in the main, these things are not available to them any more than they are to anyone else – and that the university will probably treat them in just the same way as it might treat a penniless 20-year-old. There may also be a sense – as in Averil Horse-ford's experience, in the previous chapter – that part-time students are less a part of the institution than full-timers, which can be disappointing if you are unprepared for this possibility.

As I have already noted, big educational institutions are unlikely to tailor their facilities specifically to meet your needs, and will expect you to 'fit in' around them. On the other hand, they will probably provide a wide range of facilities for you and other students to use and, whether you are working online or attending your course in person, it is worth making a bit of effort to find out what is on offer. Students who settle down and enjoy their study often find it easiest to do so by making the most of what is available to all – for example, your institution might offer well-designed websites on (for example) research ethics, 'free' courses on improving IT and design skills, reading groups both online and on campus, good support from course advisers in relation to course requirements and assignments and so on.

It is worth noting that it will probably be up to you to investigate what is available. Handbooks/websites and tutors/supervisors might be able to give you some advice, but it is quite common for students to have to find their own way around the system, when they will usually discover all sorts of interesting and unexpected facilities which no one had told them about. Libraries provide a good example of this. Most institutions will offer good library facilities and there will probably be a librarian who specializes in your field but this might not be advertised in any of the student literature. Your subject librarian might be able to provide advice on the phone or online and if you are attending your programme in person, might also be able to offer 'hands-on' support with literature and other searches. Although they are unlikely to advertise this, some libraries have budgets to buy books which they do not keep in stock and some even hold budgets which allow for books and journals which are not available online to be photocopied and sent out to students. I cannot promise that your library will offer all this, but it is worth finding out! A further example would be student support services. Universities and colleges may offer financial advice for those who are struggling to pay fees, study advice for those whose first language is not English and health services or counselling for students who are in difficulties. It would be easy to assume that these facilities do not exist for you, because you are part-time and because nobody has told you about them. However, part-time students are often full members of their college or university and have exactly the same rights as full-time undergraduates. Often, the 'basic' course handbooks and websites will not tell you about these benefits and tutors/supervisors may fail to mention what services are available simply because they are unaware that these exist.

It is worth doing a thorough web-search and (if you happen to be a part-time 'present' student) just taking some time to nose around campus and see what is about. Talking to other students who have done your course can also provide you with some handy tips. They may know about online study groups, or student support services that aren't apparent from websites. Find out what your institution has to offer, and make the most of it!

Managing on your own

Ironically, although your university might treat you as 'one of the crowd', being a part-time student can mean that you are working very much under your own steam, and this can feel quite lonely. In theory, part-time students shouldn't feel isolated at all because there are thousands of part-timers worldwide, meaning that many others are in just the same situation as you. Additionally, most universities and colleges will do their best to set up face-to-face or virtual support networks, and for some students these work very well. Unfortunately, however, for many students the experience of doing a part-time degree is one of relative remoteness from the university or college setting. Even those who are on 'present' modular courses (meaning that they are on campus for days or weeks at a time) may feel as though they are peripheral to the central activities of their institution, especially if they are older than the average undergraduate (which could apply even to students in their early 20s). Perhaps your module lasts a week or even a fortnight, but just as you feel you are getting to know your way around, it is time to leave. This can be quite intimidating – rather like standing on the edges of a group of people at a party where everyone seems to know everyone else – but *you* are not part of the inner circle. Online students might never visit their institution in person and may find it difficult to make good relationships in cyberspace. As noted earlier, these experiences do not accord with the idea of universities as social spaces in which you will study with like-minded people, and make friends for life. Creating good support networks can make a big difference to your enjoyment and success at postgraduate level. If you are a part-timer, you may have to work hard to develop these and you will also need to develop strategies for managing your own learning, some suggestions for which are outlined below.

Expecting you to take the lead

This leads me on to the final point with regard to managing your own expectations about life as a part-time student: although they should provide you with tutor/supervisor support, and with the relevant course materials, your university is unlikely to take responsibility for the success or failure of part-time students. This is because, even if they do not state this, they will probably believe that (while they will do their best to provide a high standard of teaching) *the responsibility for managing your learning lies with you*. Thus, while they might exert direct pressure on full-time students who fall behind, institutions tend to leave part-time students to their own devices. Decisions about whether you hand your work in on time, about how many hours you devote to it, and whether you go all out to achieve your full academic potential are, in the end, likely to be yours entirely. You will take the lead, and your success or otherwise on your course will be down to your own organizational skills and your intellectual ability. This will remain the case no matter how alluring the advertising materials, or how costly your course. In some respects, given that you will be awarded a degree or a diploma at the end of your studies, this principle is not unreasonable, because the person who will graduate with a qualification, and who may be employed or promoted on the basis of this, is not the awarding institution, but the student.

However, as I have already noted, it seems to me (perhaps understandably given the level of hype in some promotional materials) that this is not always obvious to students when they begin their studies. Many fee-paying part-time students vaguely imagine (if they have thought about it at all) that payment of course fees, and attendance at classes (real or virtual), will guarantee them a place at their graduation ceremony. This assumption can lead to disappointment because it is categorically not the case. The higher the degree or qualification and the more prestigious the institution, the tougher the assessment process will be – and the more you will have to push yourself to study and do well, if you are studying part-time. It is therefore important that I summarize the issues very clearly before going on to the next section.

Managing your own expectations: summary of key points

- To avoid disappointment, look beyond the advertising and check out the details of what you might expect in practice.
- Universities usually treat students collectively, but if you do your research you can usually seek out facilities which are on offer to all, but which will suit you.
- No matter what the adverts promised or how much your course costs, *you will be responsible for managing your own learning.*

Student experience

I signed up to do a postgraduate diploma in marketing at a prestigious university. The course was advertised in glossy brochures as suitable for 'executives', and it was very expensive. When we arrived we were given leather folders with the university logo embossed on the front. Sparkling water was provided in blue bottles with the university logo on the label, and classes took place in 'executive rooms'.

When it came to managing the academic work, though, I felt very much on my own. I got a bit cross about the lack of hand-outs and when I asked one lecturer for copies of his slides, he said: 'I don't provide copies of my unpublished work. You should have taken notes.' Also, the course reading list was quite limited and a bit out of date really. When I queried this, the course leader told me to go online and do my own literature search. I also remember sending a complete draft of my first assignment for comment to my supervisor. She replied that she does not read drafts as a matter of policy because it is the student's work not hers and she told me to summarize my arguments instead, then she would comment.

I remember a big fuss when one person on the course queried the date of the exams, which clashed with an expensive holiday that she had booked. She was told (in no uncertain terms) that exam dates were set well in advance and would not be altered.

Looking back on my experience, they described the course as 'executive' which in some ways it was – we had very nice facilities. But underneath all that, as far as the university was concerned, we were just students. We had to take responsibility for ourselves and fit in with their systems if we wanted to succeed. And in a way, looking back, I can understand that. After all, nobody can say that I did not earn or deserve my diploma.

(Jane, part-time postgraduate, Marketing)

How to manage your own learning

This section provides some straightforward guidelines about how a high level of self-sufficiency might be achieved, which will stand you in good stead throughout your part-time study. Below are some key steps to help you manage your own learning. These are relevant regardless of whether you are studying at a distance or whether you are a part-time 'present' student. They will be helpful to part-timers studying at all levels within the academy. I will follow these up with suggestions about how you can make the most of what your institution has to offer. In this section I provide some real-life examples, and offer ideas to get you started and keep you motivated. Some of these things might sound fairly obvious but many part-time students don't do them until it is far too late! This section will therefore cover the following issues:

- Managing your own learning and keeping up with your work.
- Getting organized.
- Sticking to your timetable.
- Incentives and building support networks.

Managing your own learning and keeping up with your work

When young undergraduate students leave home for the first time to go to university they can no longer rely on parents or teachers to 'keep tabs' on whether or not they are doing their homework. Managing to find the required time for study is something that they have to learn to do for themselves. It would be easy to assume that students who have returned to education after a break, or who have chosen to study part-time, would manage this better than full-time undergraduates.

However, Yum *et al*. (2005) interviewed 53 part-time students in eight universities in Hong Kong. Yum *et al*. discovered that the major difficulties facing most of the part-time students was the problem of finding (and putting in!) the amount of time required to succeed on their course. Most participants were juggling the demands of work, family and social life as well as personal needs such as sporting activities. Inevitably, part-time students with other commitments often put their academic work to one side while they deal with other things, only to find that weeks have flown by and they are seriously behind with their studies. If this sounds familiar to you, there might be a good reason for it. For most students, especially those who are doing their first degree, or who have been away from education for a long time, the beginning of a course can feel incredibly daunting. It can be tempting, at this point, to engage in displacement activities either at home or at work, for example tidying out the garage, a job which may have needed doing for years, but which takes on a new level of importance when compared with the need to sit down and write an assignment. You will not be alone. Even people who are very efficient with regard to their paid employment, and are never late with reports and budgets, find it extraordinarily difficult to settle down to writing essays. Resisting the temptation to do other things is a battle you need to fight and win, because getting going and settling into a routine at the outset is essential, and can make the difference between part-timers who do well and get to the end of their programme, and those who never really get started.

Essays, assignments and research plans may also be sidelined because of pressures from other people. Colleagues will lean on you to meet requirements at work, friends and relatives will remind you of your family and social obligations, but quite possibly no one will ask you whether you are going to hand your essay in on time. Furthermore, those who managed successfully to focus on social and sporting life at undergraduate level, leaving academic work until the last available minute, usually find it much more difficult to keep on top of their studies as a part-time student with more commitments than in their relatively carefree undergraduate days! It is important to avoid getting behind with your coursework, because once you have allowed a backlog to build up, it becomes very difficult to get on top of this – especially if you were pressed for time in the first place. This becomes depressing, because other students online or in the classroom will be moving ahead. They will not have time to worry about you and may not even notice if you fail to appear in your online conference room. The requirement to catch up can begin to feel overwhelming and it is at this point that many part-time students give up altogether. Although it is not easy, there are some steps you can take to avoid this scenario, which brings us back to the idea of managing your own learning – and in particular, managing and prioritizing your time. As Hendry and Farley (2004: 81) suggest, 'It is important from an early stage that you get to grips with the time issues and that you learn to manage your time effectively.'

Getting started – planning a year ahead

In order to manage your own learning and produce good work within the given timescale, you need to provide yourself with a clear idea of what your university requires of you over the next 12 months. Then you need to consider how this fits in with paid work and social commitments. Although there may be some things you cannot predict exactly, you ought to be able to factor in some 'guesstimates'. For example, a hospital manager would know that the emergency room was likely to be busier at certain times of year than others, and teachers will know when exam scripts will land on their desks, so it should be possible to plan around these events.

The first step is literally to lay out the year ahead. Don't just rely on your diary to do this, but buy or make yourself a wall planner, and ensure that assignment deadlines are represented alongside other key events in your life, so that you can see it all in front of you. If you use a computerized calendar, print it out and stick it up on the wall somewhere prominent so that you can see it at a glance, without having to go to the effort of bringing it up on screen. At this stage, you will be able to predict well in advance where the pressures are going to be, and plan accordingly. So if your assignment is due in at the same time as a major religious festival, you might want to get it ready to hand in early – or at least begin it in good time, so that you are not caught out by trying (and failing) to do everything at the last minute. Furthermore, when you are asked if you can take on additional commitments in work or home life, you will only have to glance at your year ahead calendar to see how realistic these are in relation to your academic work. Finally, assignment hand-in dates will not creep up on you, and come as a horrible shock.

Setting yourself interim goals and a detailed timetable for each assignment

Imagine you were making suggestions to a friend about how they should approach a part-time degree programme. You would *not* advise them to leave everything until the last minute, and then burn the midnight oil before submitting a poorly presented assignment. You would probably recommend regular study, tackling work bit by bit and allowing time at the end to read through before handing in. You might even ring them up or e-mail them to chivvy them along. You may not have anybody on hand to do this for you, but you can do it for yourself. Having completed a general year ahead calendar outlining what is due in when, you can set yourself *a more detailed timetable for each piece of work*. This would include organizing your assignments into manageable chunks, so that you are not working merely to the date when work should be submitted (which makes it tempting to leave everything until the end), but setting yourself some interim goals. For example, Doreen Smith, doing her masters in educational research, organized the schedule for her assignment as illustrated in the table below. Doreen thought through carefully how she would tackle each section of her assignment and by when. She built in some incentives to help spur her on.

Having made yourself a timetable, resist the temptation to hide it in a file on your computer – *print it out* and stick it up where you can see it! Having done this, think of ways of making yourself stick to it.

MONTH	LITERATURE	RESEARCH	WRITING
March Incentive for completing tasks on time: buy *Vogue* and *Glamour* magazines and read both . . .	Start reading and make notes on each book/article.	Design *and pilot* questionnaire – 4 interviewees minimum. Any changes needed?	Produce draft literature review and draft introduction.
April – take one week's leave and do fieldwork Incentive: new shoes		Undertake *and complete* research interviews.	Write up methodology section.
May Incentive: day off to play golf, lesson with pro	Do any further reading required as a result of findings.	Analyse research data and pull out key themes.	Write up findings and relate these to the relevant literature. Complete literature review, write introduction and conclusions.
June 16 HAND IN Incentive: have hair extensions and nails done			Read through carefully and edit. Check rules and ensure that work is correctly presented and does not exceed word count.

Sticking to your timetable

Once you have designed yourself a timetable, it is important to meet your own deadlines. Hendry and Farley (2004: 81) offer two reasons for why part-time students may struggle to meet deadlines. The first is that students often

. . . behave as if they have all the time in the world but as deadlines approach, they begin to experience the mounting pressure of not having enough time. This may be because when faced with a lengthy project they often do not distribute the workload and tasks evenly or appropriately over the lifetime of [the task in hand]. They may spend longer than is necessary and longer than they can afford in the earlier part of the work.

The second reason suggested by Hendry and Farley (2004: 82) is because students

> . . . may put off or postpone the necessary work and may find themselves easily distracted. They may also engage in tasks not related to the research study; for example, the student may take the opportunity to use the time set aside for research to [do something else quite different] . . . It is a common human characteristic to put off until tomorrow that which we should do today.

If the issue of procrastination sounds familiar, then try and recognize this, and start early, as in Elizabeth's case, below. As you work to your timetable, make sure that you have distributed your workload evenly and that you are not spending far too long at the beginning gathering data, or writing your introduction, leaving yourself with insufficient time at the end. If you are due to see your tutor/supervisor, don't put it off! The pressure of knowing you are due to see him/her will act as an incentive to keep going and produce some work (as in Paul's case below). (Conversely, if you cancel appointments it becomes all the more tempting to do nothing!) Begin writing at the outset, and (as in both Paul and Elizabeth's case) try to hand all work in on time, even if you feel it is not perfect. On each occasion, check with your year ahead calendar to see if your assignment timetable is feasible. For example, Doreen decided to take a week off work in April in order to do her fieldwork, but she checked that this fitted in with her schedule first, and blocked it out in her year ahead calendar.

Student experience

I am someone who procrastinates terribly so I forced myself to start early. Just taking notes from books and making myself take down the references properly was so important for me, because I knew that if I didn't do this I'd get into a mess later.

I also recognized that I had different kinds of energies and types of attention so I made sure that I did work that fitted with these. So if I was tired but needed to do some work I would just work on my bibliography. Or I would allow myself to write a bad draft that I could work up later when I had more time or was more alert. We had a clear hand-in date and time and there were well-defined 'punishments' if you didn't hand in your assignment on time. I always made sure that I got it in in time – sometimes by a matter of seconds – mostly this was just so that I didn't lose any marks. However, it was also to ensure that I didn't prolong it unnecessarily – making myself complete an assignment before the deadline was hard enough. But I feared that making myself do this when it was late and I had already lost marks would be just about impossible. So planning, starting early and keeping going was really important for me.

(Elizabeth, part-time postgraduate, Educational Psychology)

Student experience

Taking control of the diary is crucial for part-time study. I block in regular study sessions with bite-sized tasks that keep things moving. When I was doing assignments I always completed them on time and now I agree tasks with my supervisor each time we meet and treat those in the same way as I did my assignments. What sustains me in part-time study when I lose confidence is taking the initiative to visit my supervisor more, rather than less frequently, i.e. monthly, even though it means a five-hour round trip by car. That makes me do the work, instead of being tempted to focus on other things.

Part-time distance learning presents particular challenges if, like me, you live a long way from your university. It is easy to feel very isolated from what is going on. Time spent on campus, in the library, meeting staff and fellow researchers is stimulating in itself. For me, even though it adds to the cost, using a B&B overnight extends the experience hugely.

Also, investing time getting to know the doctoral programme office staff in the university is important. Supervisors will help with the academic side of things but the advice and practical support offered by the admin team is particularly helpful when you are part-time and off campus. It is amazing what they know!

(Paul, part-time PhD, Religious Studies)

Give yourself an incentive

If your assignment timetable looks feasible, think of ways in which you can persuade yourself to stick to it. For example, Doreen, a keen golfer, promised herself a day's golfing, lunch at the club and a lesson with the 'pro' if she met her self-imposed May deadline. This was something to really work towards because every time she felt like settling down to watch telly instead of getting on with her assignment, she reminded herself about the golf. Of course, this technique will only work if you are really strict with yourself. No May deadline – no golf.

Get a friend or partner to help you manage deadlines

If you know perfectly well that successful self-management of deadlines is unlikely to be one of your big strengths, and incentives won't work for you (you probably won't meet your May goal, but you'll take the golf lesson anyway), you might think of looking for a friend or colleague who will push you to keep up with your work. This might be someone on your programme (you could offer to do the same for them) or someone unconnected with your studies. If you choose the latter, you will have to be honest with them well in advance about what the deadlines are, so that they can chase you accordingly. You will also need to be honest with them as you progress their work, as the anecdote that follows demonstrates.

Joe (an academic, and a good friend) was writing a book. He recounts how his partner Beth had agreed to liaise with his publishers as things progressed in order to save him the time and hassle of dealing himself with editors' queries. At various stages in the project, Beth would press him to update her on progress and he would describe how well things were going with the book. His office was upstairs in a quiet part of the house and he always put his things away at the end of a writing session, so that they could not be seen. After one particularly difficult conversation with the publishing house, Beth came upstairs and interrupted Joe. Beth stood behind him and looked at what was on the screen. Beth was not too pleased when she read the words: 'Chapter 1'. In retrospect, Joe felt it would have been better for all concerned had he been more open with Beth, who might have been able to help him set goals and keep up with deadlines, as opposed to falling behind to the point where he felt under serious pressure.

Building good student networks

One advantage held by full-time students is the automatic peer pressure experienced when all are working to a given timetable, and likely to be in regular contact. There is nothing like realizing that your friend has made good progress with her assignment, or her research, to spur you on to do some work of your own! At times, part-time students may feel very isolated. Even if you are 'present' in groups for modules at the university, once you are back home and working alone, the prospect of producing assignments, working on a dissertation or doing PhD research can feel very lonely. If your university has not already set up web-boards where you can communicate online, there is nothing to stop you doing this for yourselves. Regular contact with others will give you a sense of how well you are keeping up with course commitments and will also give you someone to turn to if you are stuck, or just fed-up (see Elizabeth's example, below).

Student experience

It was really tough sometimes to balance out work commitments and the course commitments. The best thing for me during times like this was to email my fellow students. Even if they couldn't do anything it was good just to speak to people who were in the same boat. Friends who weren't doing the course were great but they didn't ever really understand the pressures of doing the course. We set up a virtual chatroom so that we could talk about assignments and share resources. Often when I was feeling under pressure, it would transpire that everyone else was feeling the same. It didn't make the problems go away but it felt like I wasn't alone.

(Elizabeth, part-time postgraduate, Educational Psychology)

Prioritizing yourself and your studies

Doing well in a part-time degree means making yourself, and your studies, the priority. This might be easier said than done if you have a busy job and family or friends who are accustomed to having a given share of your time. Your paid work will always put pressure on you to do more (whether this is imposed by others or self-imposed) and family and friends, while they might accept that you are tied up with your paid work, may resent it when your 'spare' time is given up to studying. But it is essential that you give some practical thought to how you are going to prevent your studies from always being pushed to the back of the queue. You can begin by working out an estimate of how much study time you will need each week. A good way of doing this, if your college does not give you any suggestions, is to contact one or two others who have undertaken the course in previous years and see if they can give you some idea. If you cannot get hold of this information, a good 'rough' guide in my view would be 10–12 hours per week for a masters or undergraduate degree, perhaps a bit less for a postgraduate diploma or certificate and *significantly more* for an MPhil/MLitt, or a PhD. You will also need significantly more than 10–12 hours if you are aiming for a distinction grade in your masters or undergraduate degree. Probably, part-time PhD students and aspiring distinction students at masters or undergraduate level are looking at around 25 hours of study per week. Once you have a good idea of how much time is required you are in a position to work out where this is going to come from. This is a serious question. 10–12 hours per week means you need to free up 40–50 hours per month, which is the equivalent of 5–6 working days. Whether you choose to work in the evenings or at weekends, or to negotiate some study leave, your studies will inevitably impinge on your paid work, family and social life. Somehow – certainly if you are working at masters level or above – you are going to have to work out ways of managing this.

Ring-fencing time for study

As far as paid employment is concerned, finding the time can be a challenge wherever you are in the employment hierarchy. If you are a senior nurse working on a busy hospital ward, for example, it can be difficult to refuse urgent requests to come into work during periods of short-staffing, especially if these are accompanied by the suggestion that patient care may suffer due to your lack of cooperation. If you are the head of your department or organization it can also be difficult to allow yourself the luxury of being away from the workplace, leaving others in charge, especially during times of crisis. The problem is that, in relation to paid work, whatever your level of seniority, there will always be some crisis or project which requires your immediate attention. Somehow, you need to make the mental step of believing that your part-time study is more important than almost everything else on your agenda. This is not an easy thing to do. Many of us have been brought up to believe that paid work is of great importance. Writers on management, and on stress, such as Lewis and Cooper (1999), and Collinson and Collinson (2004), observe that, in the present climate of the 'long hours' culture, there is often pressure to be visible at work. 'Presenteeism' – the need to be seen in the office after hours and during your 'own' time – is associated with fears of redundancy or limited career progression for those who appear to be any-thing other than wholly committed to their employment. The guilt and anxiety that part-time students experience with regard to continuing their studies in the face of the pressure to be seen to be working long hours can be a major block to making progress with their academic work. Furthermore, as Hendry and Farley (2004: 2) observe, part-time students who are employed have the additional problem of being unable to 'immerse' themselves in their studies. Every time they pick up their studies, following periods where they have been caught up in the pressures of their 'day job', part-time students 'have to use up some of their time allocation by simply "tuning in" and reminding themselves where they are [up to]'. Often it helps to have thought through the reasons – both at work and in your private life – behind your decision to make yourself, and your part-time study, the priority. This not only provides you with the relevant explanations when questioned by others. It can also help you feel more convinced about your decision to prioritize part-time study.

Ideally, the arguments in favour of dedicating time to study (which might otherwise have been dedicated to paid work) would be formulated before the start of a course. Life being what it is, however, it is often not until the start of the programme, when the pressure is felt, that students begin to think about how they are going to justify the amount of time they need to spend on their academic work. The mindset that your part-time course takes precedence over other things is fundamental to your success, because you can be sure that no one else will take this view, so the decision to prioritize yourself and your studies has to come from you, and you alone. You may, however (especially if your assignments/dissertation are work-based), be able to engage line managers and colleagues in what you are doing, so that they can see the organizational benefits of your part-time study. This would also have the advantage of your ideas becoming part of organizational practice, and might mean it is easier to convince colleagues of your need to prioritize part-time study, as in Elizabeth's example, below. Some further suggestions about how you might argue your case are included after Elizabeth's example.

Student experience

One of the things I did was to try to feed in my work to the department. So I involved my line manager in scoping some of my assignments and involved other people in the organization in the research. This meant that, although I changed more than everyone else, at least some of the ideas I was working with circulated a bit in the organization, and others began to see my part-time study as important and relevant to what we are all doing.

(Elizabeth, part-time postgraduate, Human Resources Management)

Arguments for prioritizing your study in the context of paid work

- *If employers are paying for you to do the course:* 'This is your investment. I want to ensure that I provide the best possible return, so I will need some additional study time.'
- Once I have completed my course of study I will have more to offer the organization in terms of confidence and enhanced managerial (or other) ability.
- When individuals are engaged in continuing professional development, the whole organization benefits.

Practical ways of negotiating the time you need

In a work environment, people prefer it if their colleagues are available and 'on call' at all times. It is often necessary to be clear about what you can and can't do – and then stick to it, as with Alex and Erin's examples below. At least everybody then knows where they are. If there is a 'regular' aspect to your study schedule, colleagues will usually accept it – even if you have to remind them of what has been agreed, and even if they are unenthusiastic about it:

- I will need to leave at 6 pm on Wednesdays and Thursdays from now on. If you need me on those days, can we schedule meetings no later than 4 pm? However, I can be available on Monday and Tuesday evenings if need be.
- It would be much better for everyone if we take a planned approach to study, rather than me having to take huge chunks of annual leave at short notice, when I am under pressure.

Student experience

I am the Chief Executive Officer of a county council. I have a teenage family. I have worked out a system whereby it is possible for me to be away from the workplace for short periods of time while others deputize for me, which is good experience for them. Although I am fairly pressured as regards paid work, I am well organized and clear about my work–life boundaries. I formally schedule in time to work on my degree. In this way, I do not find myself trying to cram everything into the last minute. I am consistent in my argument that the council's investment in me is a long-term one, which will benefit the organization because it keeps me at the forefront of social policy, which I can apply to practice, giving my council a leading edge. The quality of my work has been consistently high and I have shared feedback and progress with one of the councillors, who is my mentor. This helps to keep everyone on board and so far I have managed well.

(Alex, part-time PhD in Social Policy)

Student experience

I am a nurse manager in a busy hospital, doing a part-time distance learning degree in advanced nursing. I live on my own and I have found it more difficult to be assertive, partly because I am not that senior and partly because people look to me to fill in when we are short on the wards because I don't have any family to go home to. In the past I used to do this but now I need the time for study so I use lieu time and holiday time to do my assignments. I book this off in chunks well in advance, inform my colleagues and then arrange to go and stay in a fishing lodge some distance from the hospital where I settle down with a computer and get on with my academic work. The lodge has to be booked and paid for six weeks before I arrive. This makes it easier for me to justify (both to my employer and to myself) saying 'no' to last-minute requests to come into work, no matter how urgent these may be, or how guilty I feel about refusing.

(Erin, part-time masters in Advanced Nursing Practice)

Part-time study and home life

Of course, you will have good reasons why you need to create some time for studying by taking it from both your paid work and your private life, but (as we shall see below) arguments can be more difficult to formulate and apply to private life than to employment. As far as friends and family are concerned, 'ring-fencing' time for private study can be even more complicated. Children, friends and relatives may be unsympathetic to your desire to reject their company in favour of a computer screen, and partners can get seriously fed up if they feel they are playing second fiddle to textbooks and the internet. Once again, although it might seem logical to have talked through the question of 'time' with friends and family, this is often not negotiated until after the programme of study is underway. This is sometimes because it can be quite hard to get an idea of what is involved in a course before starting. When I teach study skills at the beginning of part-time programmes at my own university, the most commonly asked question (after 'do people ever fail this programme?') is 'how many hours am I going to need to study each week in order to pass?'

If you have read the section on 'Prioritising yourself and your studies' on page 49, you will already know that the answer given to the latter question is that most students will need to spend an average of 10–12 hours per week on part-time study (especially if they are working at postgraduate level). Those aiming to do really well will need to find around 25 hours per week. This can come as a shock to some students, and I am aware that many can face problems when they go home and explain it to friends and partners.

Sometimes, where hobbies are concerned, the only option is to disappoint. For me – when doing my MBA – this meant giving up amateur dramatics and, specifically, the opportunity to play the female lead in a play. Disappointment on all sides at the outset seemed better than failing to do either job well – or, worse still, having to give up halfway through! Where family and friends are concerned, the pressures can be really tough. The research of Kember *et al.* (2005) suggests that many part-time students find it difficult enough to adapt employment practices in order to free up time for part-time study. Even where employment and part-time study are, theoretically, designed to be integrated, students often find that study time is nevertheless 'squeezed' as paid work claims the lion's share. The inevitable consequence of the difficulties involved in taking time out of paid work and reallocating this for part-time study means that time for social or family activities is reduced. Thus, the sacrifices associated with part-time study are made not only by the student but by those close to her/him. Students who seem to achieve the best compromises between family/social and study time are those who agree clear boundaries and then stick to them. For example, agreements that part-time study will not impinge on summer holidays abroad should mean just that. No textbooks, no computers and an agreed period of 'time out' when everyone can relax. If you are in for the 'long haul', like Jack (who has now embarked on his PhD as a part-time student), this is really important.

Student experience

My study lasted three years. Three long, family-impacting, weekend-losing years. Whilst I enjoyed the study from start to end, and never doubted the fact that I would complete the course, the real strain is felt by your family. The worst time: sunny Saturdays and Sundays. Having my 2-year-old daughter ask me to come and play in the garden and have to say no is hard. Really hard. If you have a family, then the family bears the stress of your study more than you do. This is often overlooked by many students. If you study, then everyone studies. If you want to be successful, you *need* this support, else you will be quickly choosing between study and family and that is a lose–lose option if there ever was one.

(Jack, part-time postgraduate, MBA)

The benefit of sticking to your side of the bargain is that others will be more likely to stick to theirs. Breaking your side of the bargain might well mean that you lose support with regard to the time your significant others *had* agreed was yours for studying in. Many students have noted the inadvisability of complaining about the pressures of part-time study to close family members. One student, whose experiences are quoted earlier in this book, said: 'Mostly my husband tolerates it. But every so often he just goes off on one.' See also Paul's experience below, and remember that your part-time study might adversely affect others in your household/social circle, and that they may feel they have more cause for complaint than you do.

Student experience

My wife isn't over-sympathetic to my whinging about the research project – 'it's your choice', she says! However, she appreciates it's something I'm keen to achieve and she's very supportive (and a critical proof reader) of my work.

My grown-up daughter, who has successfully completed part-time study herself, understands the demands and has the knack of giving encouragement just when it's most needed. But work, home life and part-time study just have to be a *ménage à trois*. Home life cannot be neglected at the expense of your research, so you just have to work out ways of dealing with this

(Paul, part-time PhD, Religious Studies)

Part-time study and the threat to existing personal relationships

Finally, if you are facing real opposition from family and friends with regard to your part-time study, it is worth considering that they may see your part-time study as a potential threat, which could change you as a person and may therefore threaten existing relationships. It is acknowledged that higher education changes the individuals who engage in it (Hatt *et al.* 1999) and, often, the motivation for doing a degree in the first place is *because* of the opportunities for personal development that higher education provides. For some students, however, part-time study may cause unanticipated problems because, while *you* may be developing personally, your immediate social world may have remained pretty much the same. Both you and those close to you may find this hard to deal with. Of course, this book cannot resolve these problems for you – and it is recognized that you may be doing your degree specifically *in order* to facilitate major life changes like Linda, below. However, if those close to you seem unsupportive and unenthusiastic about what you are doing, and if you had not anticipated this, it may be worth considering the reasons behind their worries. If you are planning to take them with you on your personal journey, it might be worth talking this through, and trying to offer them some reassurance.

Student experience

There is no doubt that education does change you. And I am a different person since I did my IT degree. I was quite shy and doing secretarial jobs before. But I was always really good with the IT and that was appreciated in emergencies when there was no one in the IT team available. So I got on this IT course by chance because someone else dropped out and the place was already paid for. It was a real eye-opener. Because although a lot of the others on the course were earning more than me, I was better than them. So I thought: I can do this, so I worked really hard and got on with it. This made a big difference to my confidence and before long I was looking round for a proper IT job [elsewhere]. And I got a better job and at the interview I said I wanted some time and money to do my degree. Then I got another step up, so financially I earn far more than before and I am a far more confident person.

But there was some fall-out. My partner at that time liked the idea of me earning less than him. He took me a bit for granted and he thought I would put up with just about anything. When I got a better job he didn't know how to take it and I am sure he thought I wouldn't last. But then I got this even better job doing systems management, and I earn really good money now and he hated that; he said it's the job or me. So I broke up with him. But I wouldn't go back. I'd far rather be me now than me before, and I am now looking at starting my own business.

(Linda, joint part-time MSc, IT Management)

Joint part-time study

For those who are in long-term partnerships and where *both* of you are interested in academic study, a quid pro quo can provide a way of dealing with the time commitment. One apparent trend among part-time students is for couples to take turns at postgraduate study, meaning that the person 'holding the fort' – looking after the home and family responsibilities – knows that this is only for a given period of time, and that their opportunity to claim space for study and personal development is round the corner. Some couples decide to 'go for it' and both study at the same time, even, in some cases, on the same course. This can work well if there are no dependants, or if there are children of an age when study is part of their lives too, and they are working towards high school or university qualifications, giving a sense that the whole household is 'in the same boat' and that studying is more than just an unpleasant part of growing up, imposed on reluctant teenagers by parents who have forgotten what it feels like! The concept of part-time study when you are a single parent, or when two partners/childcarers in a household are studying, is more difficult if children are very small – but may not be impossible (see Annabel's experience below).

Student experiences

Cath and Joe – taking turns
We have children aged 5, 8 and 11 and we both have jobs as senior managers. Over the past seven years, we have each obtained an MA, and Cath has just completed an MPhil degree. And Joe is due to start on exactly the same programme in September. We're talking over a long time of course, but that is OK because it feels fair. Since we began studying, the part-time parent–student has at each stage worked on her/his degree for one uninterrupted day over each weekend, while the non-studying parent entertains the children. Then work is done in the evening – the one studying goes off and does their own thing and the one taking time out sits down with the kids and helps them sort out homework and so on.

Chris and Matt – studying jointly
We have two teenage boys of 14 and 16. Both of us are undertaking masters degrees in Educational Research part-time, and study periods for the whole household have been agreed. The boys like the feeling that they are not alone in having to sit down and do course work even when it's nice outside.

Annabel – single parent
I am on my own with boys of 4 and 6. I am firm about early bedtimes for my sons and, no matter how tired I am, I do at least two hours' academic work on weekday nights. It is hard trying to manage all this combined with my job as an IT manager in a hospital, but somehow I get by and I always take Sunday off from paid work and study so I can spend time with the children.

Part-time study and the single student

Being single, or without dependent children, does not necessarily place you in a better position to study part-time. Employers, friends and family might expect more from you if you have no immediate family ties and you might find it difficult to manage their expectations. I remember doing my Certificate in Health Services Management while working as an NHS manager. I loved my job, did not have a partner or children at that time and had become used to working very long hours. It was sometimes difficult to claw back the time I needed for study, because colleagues had come to take for granted the fact that I would be generally available and would not mind evening work. Ramsay and Letherby (2006) observe that, for women in particular, there may be expectations that those without children will work long hours and that, having no children of their own to look after, they will also provide pastoral care in the workplace. Gina, below, observes how her two sisters took for granted that she would care for her mother after her father's death. Gina had to be quite assertive to claim time for herself in order to pursue her part-time studies. See also Dan's experience on page 124.

Student experience

I am doing a degree in English and I hope one day to be able to teach. After Dad died I found it really hard. I live nearer Mum than my two sisters and they both have young families. And I was happy to spend time with Mum and give her my support, but she became very dependent. But I did start to feel a bit resentful when I realized that Ruth and June were just assuming that this was 'my' job and that they were let out of it because they had kids. They really did little to help and in the end I just had to say to Mum how desperate I was feeling, and be firm about spending at least a couple of evenings and every other weekend on my own.

(Gina, part-time undergraduate, English)

Strategies for managing your own learning: summary of key points

- Finding the time to manage part-time study alongside other commitments is tough. You need to plan ahead both in the long term and also in the short term, setting yourself interim goals as you complete each assignment/ research task.
- You must find ways of sticking to your timetable. Resist the temptation to

procrastinate by giving yourself incentives, or getting a partner or friend to help you manage your deadlines.

- Whether learning at a distance or by part-time attendance at university, you must build up good student networks to avoid feeling isolated.
- Prioritizing yourself and your studies is vital. Where possible, ring-fence time for study from paid work and be firm about this.
- If you are single, be assertive about taking the time you need for part-time study.
- If you have a family, appreciate that they may be making sacrifices to support your part-time study, so be sure to honour whatever agreements you have made with them.

Part-time study and overseas students

How do you cope with part-time study if you are an overseas student? Are the needs and experiences of 'overseas' or 'international' students likely to be quantifiably different from those of 'local' students? And when writers consider the position of 'overseas students', who exactly are they talking about?

There is some literature on Western students studying in non-Western contexts. This includes Auger and Overby's (2005) study of the Hopkins Nanjing University Center for Chinese and American studies, which brings together Chinese and American students, and where American students are immersed in Chinese culture and taught in Chinese. In addition, Hashim and Zhiliang (2003) considered the experiences of African and Western students studying in China. However, much of what is written in the education journals is concerned with the experiences of non-Western students studying in European, North American or Australian institutions. Furthermore, the majority of the literature on studying overseas focuses on the traditional notion of students engaging in *full-time* study while resident in a 'foreign' country. Those studying the experiences of overseas students consider factors such as homesickness and the cross-cultural adjustments that need to be made by partners and family members (De Verthelyi 1995).

Some writers argue that, for students from non-Western countries, the Western education system can be a mystery and difficult to understand. It is suggested that Western academic tenets of inquiry, challenge, argument and debate are not the same as those developed in many countries in Asia or the Far East, where academic pedagogies tend to be based on instruction, with an emphasis on the unquestioning digestion of large amounts of material, and deference to faculty. In such a context, it is argued that 'overseas' or 'international' students are more likely to have difficulties engaging with the expectations and language of Western institutions than those who have previously been educated in Europe, Australia or North America (Littlemore 2001).

Often, in this context, it is suggested that overseas students are disadvantaged when trying to compete equally with Western students because of unfamiliarity with the English language and because they lack confidence in group work. For example, Wright and Lander (2003) looked at group work among 72 male undergraduate engineering students from three ethnic cohorts in an Australian university setting (Australian-born, Anglo-European, and overseas-born South East Asian students). The writers concluded that the South East Asian students were inhibited in terms of their verbal participation when with Australian students. Littlemore (2001) considers how overseas students cope with English language in class, focusing on the use of metaphor in university lectures, and the problems that this may cause for students whose first language is not English. Littlemore suggests that overseas students often interpret metaphors literally, and in doing this, misunderstand both the main points of a lecture and the lecturer's viewpoint. Chan (1999) suggests that Western faculty designing courses fail to understand the Chinese education system. Chan argues that this leads to problems both for faculty and for students, as Chinese students find it hard to challenge and think creatively, having been conditioned by years of learning by rote. It has also been suggested that non-Western students, studying in Western institutions, are more likely to struggle with the concept of plagiarism than are the 'home' group. However, this argument is firmly challenged by Le Ha (2006) and it is also, increasingly, accepted by scholars that plagiarism is a 'culturally loaded concept' (Leask 2006).

Some writers express concern that some Western institutions may regard overseas students in financial terms and 'not as members of a scholarly community' (Habu 2000: 43). Others express the view that both students and tutors/supervisors may find that they encounter difficulties due to 'differences in culture, language and expectations' (Sakthivel 2003: 217), but argue that both students and faculty benefit from the cross-cultural experience. Sakthivel, for example, suggests that 'Although demanding, studying as an overseas student can ultimately be enlightening and invaluable' (Sakthivel 2003: 217). Hashim and Zhiliang (2003: 218) conclude that there is a 'need for cross-cultural orientation' for any student during a 'study abroad' experience, and that this will 'offer them an opportunity to learn and grow'.

There are probably two important issues to consider in relation to these views. First, all the research on overseas study discussed here is investigating the problems faced by students living and studying *full-time* in an unfamiliar country without close friends and family nearby (or, conversely, perhaps with the responsibility for unhappy partners who have also moved to the country of study and may feel homesick, lonely and bored (De Verthelyi 1995)). Obviously, the situation for overseas students studying at a distance, like Jason, who shared his experiences in Chapter 1, or attending university for short stretches as 'present students', like Eli, below, might be quite different from the situation experienced by those living away from their home country. It is difficult, therefore, to know how far the wealth of existing research on 'full-time' overseas students applies to those studying part-time. It is also hard to know how far the experiences of part-time overseas students might vary depending on their own ethnic background and the cultural context of their chosen country of study.

The second issue to consider is the suggestion, by some writers, that the view of overseas students as uniformly disadvantaged and inhibited from verbal participation and challenge is (to say the least) narrow, and might depend very much on individual circumstances. Habu (2000) observed that the motivation and experiences of Japanese (full-time) women students in Britain varied widely. Some women felt that their presence in their British institutions was 'merely tolerated and they were not encouraged in their academic endeavours'. Others, however, loved their experience. They happily and quickly integrated into their institution, and felt that overseas study offered them a chance to develop their analytical abilities in a different global context. Habu attributes these differences to the possibility that some institutions may fail to make suitable provision for overseas students because they are so caught up in the idea of overseas students as a source of income that they have lost sight of the mutual advantages of cross-cultural study. Sakthivel (2003), however, implies that any such structural problems may be overcome to the benefit both of students and faculty.

What problems might you face if you are registered part-time and overseas?

What does all this say about the issues that you will face if you are registered part-time and overseas? One thing that seems clear is that there is a need for further research on the problems confronting part-time overseas students, since most of the existing research focuses on the issues faced by full-time resident students. This suggests that there might be some things which are specific to you, and to the country where you are living, of which your lecturers might be unaware. It might be helpful if you explain these at the outset to faculty, because while it is reasonable to suppose that university staff might have picked up on the published debates about *full-time* overseas study, they may be less aware of the problems faced by *part-time* overseas students – such as, for example, the practical difficulties experienced by Eli, below. Eli was not able to register on a distance learning programme because of cuts to the electricity supply in his home country, Nigeria. Instead, he registered as a part-time present student in the UK. Eli enjoyed the taught element of the course but found the written assignments difficult. This was *not* due to misunderstandings about the English language, such as the use of metaphor, as described earlier! Eli's spoken and written English was perfect. However, the cultural context in which the lecturers and other students were working was one of Western privilege, where electricity rarely failed and course members could be in regular e-mail contact in between taught modules. Eli's experience, when he went home to Nigeria, was that as many as three weeks could go by without proper electricity supplies. This affected his abilities to produce written work on time and also meant that he sometimes felt isolated from other students.

Student experience

Attending course modules for two years involved me in extensive travel between my homeland of Nigeria and the UK. I did not mind this, as I was able to fit it in with business arrangements and with family – some of my children were studying in England. However, when I went back to Nigeria, it was a different story. Most of the students on my course were British and they cannot imagine what it is like to be without electricity, not just for an hour or two, but maybe for weeks on end.

So of course, when this happened, and we had no electricity, I could not access the library database, I could not type up my assignments and I could not send or receive e-mails. This made me feel a bit isolated from the others, who could contact one another if they were stuck or just wanted an online chat. It also meant that although I tried very hard to keep up, I did get behind with my work. Even if I had managed to produce an assignment, I often had to write this by hand and then try and find some way of typing it, or getting it typed, while the module was running. After the taught part of the course was finished, I was three essays behind which was quite depressing. Although I don't think they could have really understood what it is like in Nigeria, the course tutors accepted how difficult it was for me and let me catch up in my own time.

But I realized that I could not do this from Nigeria, so I had to get myself a place in England near to the university and just get my head down and write as much as I could while I was there, with the facilities of electricity and a computer that worked. Eventually I managed to catch up and I passed my course. But I don't think you can underestimate the difficulties of studying part-time in a Western country when you are from Nigeria. We are talking time and the expense involved in travel and being resident in the UK at least while you are trying to produce your written work!

(Eli, part-time postgraduate, Management)

In a context such as Eli's, it may be that you feel you need some personal time with your course tutor/supervisor so that you can work out a way for yourself and your faculty to manage this issue, either face-to-face or online. You should ask for this as soon as you feel you need it (don't let the problems build up), being as specific as you can about what you require and why. For any student seeking extra, one-to-one time from faculty – whether they are studying home or overseas – the response is most likely to be positive if you are able to request time in advance and explain your agenda. So, for example, if you are a part-time present student you might make your request to spend an hour with a course tutor/supervisor *in advance of the beginning of your module*. This gives him or her the opportunity to schedule this into the timetable and to give the issue some thought. If you are studying online you might write and carefully outline the issue with which you want help, suggesting a reasonable timeframe (perhaps a fortnight) in which you would like a reply.

If there does not appear to be anyone on your programme who originates from the same ethnic background as yourself, and if you would like to be in touch with someone (especially if you are finding it difficult to integrate with your course and other students), it is worth asking your tutor/supervisor or course administrator to see if anyone else from your country of residence is doing or has done your course. Failing that, you could ask your institution to find out whether there are students in a similar situation to yours on other courses, and with whom they could put you in touch.

Overseas, or international, students: summary of key points

- Much of the research on studying overseas is concerned with the experiences of full-time students and this does not address some of the problems faced by those studying part-time overseas. If there are particular problems that are worrying you, therefore, it is well worth explaining these to course tutors/supervisors, who may be unaware of the issues.
- Assumptions that non-Western students from overseas may struggle in Western contexts have been challenged. How well students integrate may depend both on the individual student and also on how well individual universities are geared up to meet the needs of overseas or international students.
- Problems faced by some international or overseas students might be practical – such as the difficulties of studying online for those resident in countries where electricity supplies are unreliable.

Working in groups

Although I have already noted that part-time students can feel isolated there are, conversely, times when you might be required to work intensively with others.

Ironically, although students often find the loneliness of part-time study difficult, group work can provide its own challenges. This is because working as part of a learning set or study group (whether face-to-face or online) requires a different approach from the mindset needed to motivate yourself when working alone. For part-time present students, group work is likely to be an integral part of your course. You might be allocated a student study group when you begin, and could be expected to continue working with the same people throughout. Part-time PhD students (although they could usually expect some one-to-one supervision) may be assigned research learning sets, either when they attend university, or online. Those who engage in distance learning but attend summer schools will find themselves undertaking some group tasks face-to-face, and there may be elements of group work online included as part of the curriculum.

There can be long-term benefits from developing your communication and teamwork skills through academic group working at all levels – from undergraduate to PhD. The chance to bounce around ideas and get feedback from course colleagues is advantageous to everyone's work. Feelings of isolation are reduced and groups which do successfully manage to share ideas often find that their thoughts are clearer, following the chance to talk things through. As Talbot (2003: 78) argues:

> Although working with others on some aspects of your course-work is perhaps more difficult, and certainly different, [perhaps especially] when studying at a distance, for some courses you may still need to demonstrate that you possess an appropriate set of skills to do so. Learning to work cooperatively and collaboratively with others to complete a project . . . can bring benefits to all group participants since it can reduce the workload of individuals and bring fresh ideas and perspectives to group members. Group working can help you learn more effectively because you will be challenged about your own ideas.

Worries about group work

Often, students who are used to working in teams as part of their 'day job' find it hard to work in academic study groups, and student group work often causes tensions. Probably the best tip for reducing group conflict is to deal with issues as they arise. It is tempting to put off dealing with problems in the hopes that they might just blow over. Sometimes this might work. However, if group problems are getting in the way of academic study, they often get worse, not better and therefore need to be addressed by group members.

Tensions are often caused because – although few people want to admit this – they are worried that others in the group might 'know' more than they do, and that their lack of academic knowledge might be exposed in the group setting. If this particular concern rings a bell, you can guarantee that you will not be the only group member who is worrying about it. Be reassured that everyone will have gaps in their knowledge, and if you pool your resources, everyone will benefit. A further worry is that other group members might appropriate your ideas. When you reach the research stage, you do need to be careful about protecting your own work (see pages 104–7). However, most group members will wish to approach assignments/research projects in their own way, which makes plagiarism of your work a relatively low risk. If you are sharing written work, you can still be cautious, naming and dating everything that you circulate, and keeping a record of electronic correspondence. Conversely, the sharing of ideas can cause students to fear they might *unintentionally* plagiarize the work of others. If you are really concerned about this, you can keep records of online discussions, so you will be able to trace conversations and work out who said what, and when. If you are working face-to-face, and feel unsure, then you could keep notes of group discussions (even if only on a white board or flip chart) and write down the initials of group members next to the suggestions that they have made, so that at the end you all know who has contributed which ideas.

Dealing with conflict within the group

Most groups experience conflict at some point, especially if they are expected to spend intensive residential periods working closely together. It may well be the case that you find yourself working with others you do not like. Sometimes, even people you are quite fond of may nevertheless be challenging to work with, and when disagreements have occurred between group members it can be difficult to move forward. However, groups do overcome tensions if they are willing to work at things.

Sometimes, conflict can be minimized if members think about, and talk through, what they believe to be the function of the group. Are you all in agreement about what the group is supposed to be doing? Or do some members have higher expectations than others? Are some members guilty of excluding, or moving forward without, the others? Or does one group member appear to be 'taking over', when the role of group leader has never been discussed? Conversely, has someone disappeared from your online group, or failed to turn up for face-to-face meetings? Or is one member failing to pull their weight? It is helpful if you can focus on group problems and processes in the context of the academic task in hand. For example, perhaps there are occasions when you do need a project leader, and maybe some group members would like to try their hand at this.

Group disagreements are often sparked off because 'fair shares' have not been agreed. Tensions may be eased if roles and responsibilities are regularly negotiated, and re-negotiated, so that a sense of equitability can be established. In this context, upsets are less likely to occur if you can focus on the strong points offered by group members, as opposed to getting cross about one another's failings. For example, a group member who is a poor timekeeper might be highly creative and able to offer exciting and original ideas.

Major, or longer-term problems within the group setting

What if group tensions are long-term, or you feel as if they are beyond the group's (or your) capacity to tackle? In this section I address the issues of interpersonal conflict within groups; the problem of feeling that you are doing the lion's share of the work; the difficulty of being the 'non-conformist' member of a group, and the sense that you feel excluded due to your gender, or ethnic background. These problems might be more serious for groups who are expected to work together over long periods, and where faculty has defined the membership, than for students working on very short-term projects, where the end is in sight.

If you are a part-time student, it is not unusual for study groups to be established for the duration of a course, which may involve working closely for a whole year (or worse, for several years!). In such circumstances (as, for example, in Jenna's group, below), if problems cannot be resolved within the group it is probably wise to approach your course tutor/supervisor to ask for help. There is no guarantee that they will provide a solution (or, if they do take action, that this will provide the solution you want). However, at least they will understand that projects are being undertaken in the context of difficult group dynamics. They may also feel it appropriate, in some circumstances, to change group membership, or tasks. Jenna's experience suggests an occasion when (although the problems might have been difficult to share with faculty) a more open approach on the part of the group could have been helpful, and might have avoided an unhappy year for all in Jenna's group.

Student experience

I was a part-time student doing a degree in Human Resource Management which I was so looking forward to. This meant that we were 'present' at the university for several days at a time, staying overnight and working very closely together in groups of six for a whole year. We were doing case studies together before (thankfully) moving into different groups for our dissertations. In my group there were three men and three women and right from the start, one of the men was very obviously chasing one of the women. They started a relationship and it was all very intense, but then he found out that she was married and ended things suddenly. He said she should have told him; she thought it was his fault because he had never asked about her circumstances. I think they were both angry and embarrassed and she was probably also I think really worried that her partner might find out.

In the whole year nobody ever spoke about this within the group and we all tried to focus on the case studies that we had been set. But there was a lot of conflict between us, always with the men pitted against the women. And the ex-couple would do anything to avoid speaking to one another, or even being in the same room if they could avoid it. And the whole time it felt like he was watching what she did and if he could say something nasty about 'women' he would, looking straight at her. I don't think the lecturers knew what to make of us and they tried all this facilitating and team-building stuff to try and get us to work together better, which obviously didn't work. And of course, nobody ever told them what had started it. But it made for some very difficult times within the group, and in a way it spoilt the year. I kind of wonder now what would have happened if someone had told them from the beginning what the problem was. Looking back I would have loved to have moved to another group. I wish I had confided in the course director, and asked to do just that.

(Jenna, part-time postgraduate, Human Resource Management)

Doing more than my fair share

What if you feel, like Nick, below, that you are doing more than your fair share of group work? It is not uncommon for study groups to fall into a pattern whereby it is assumed that the keenest member of the group will carry a heavier share of the workload than the others. This can be problematic if the keenest member of the group happens to be you! This can occur by accident, with your initial enthusiasm making it easy for others to sit back and let you get on with things, while they are socializing, or phoning the office! One option for Nick (which, as he explains, he could have tried earlier) would have been to call a group meeting and say how he felt. He could then have asked for a more even share of the library work. This would have benefited everyone because, while it must have been very convenient for other group members just to let Nick get on with putting together a list of references, it is possible that they did not realize how much time he was spending on this. Furthermore, by allowing Nick to do all the work, the group were effectively doing themselves out of the experience of undertaking their own literature search.

While you do not *need* to do more than your fair share of group work, it might be important to recognize that everyone works at a different pace, and to different ends. If you are aiming for a distinction grade, you might have to accept that others in your group will not wish to invest as many hours in study as you do. Other group members might be perfectly content to work out what they need to do to achieve passable grades, leaving them with more time free for paid work, or family/friends, than you.

Student experience

All of us are/were engineering types doing this management course and I was really keen right from the start of our course. But the others weren't that bothered because to be honest they are more interested in engineering. We were residential for a week at a time and we also did group work online. Our assignments were assessed individually but they were all the same and we did a lot of case work as a group. I did not have quite the level of home commitments that some of the others did. I had a demanding job but no kids or anything which some of the other blokes, and one girl, did.

And I really wanted to make a go of this; I wanted top marks, not because I wanted to do better than them, more as a sort of personal best. So when we were given each assignment I would set to right away, reading, taking notes, getting references and so on. And from the beginning, I would mail these to the rest of the group, even with my jottings attached. I supposed I had some vague thoughts that we would all share and they would do the same for me and we could pool our knowledge. I don't know how long it took me to realize things weren't quite working like this, but most of the rest of them were just reading the course texts and relying on me to provide all the rest of the references rather than reading things themselves. There was a point where I got really fed up with this.

But I also admit that maybe it happened because I didn't deal with it earlier. I never said to the others to do a bit more for themselves. It was like I became the resident expert and they all took it for granted. In the end it sorted itself out. We moved on to the dissertation and I started to use some quite philosophical readings. This was of little interest to the others in my group – everyone else was doing more conventional things – so I was able to move on without having to have a big row. But looking back, I wish I had said something about it earlier.

(Nick, part-time postgraduate, MBA)

What if you are the non-conformist member of your group?

It is apparent that Nick approached his studies differently from the others in his group. What if you do not obviously 'fit' with the others in your study group, or your class as a whole? What if your ideas or your politics make you feel 'out of place'? All groups develop 'ground rules', even if these are never articulated. And often a group will have at least one 'non-conformist' member who cannot, or does not wish to, accede to the majority way of doing things. Many of us experience times in our lives when we feel that we do not 'fit in' (most people can remember at least one incident from school days!).

It is important to remember that non-conformists are not necessarily 'wrong' but may be change agents, or thinkers who are ahead of their time. Gatrell and Turnbull (2003) make the point that Martin Luther King and Emmeline Pankhurst, whose politics made a difference to the lives of many people, were both non-conformists. Sometimes, non-conformists do not 'fit in' because they draw attention to things that others may prefer to overlook (such as matters relating to class, gender or ethnicity). Non-conformists often seek change, which will be unpopular with those who are perfectly happy with the way things are at the moment. If you find yourself in the position where you are the 'non-conformist', you need to find a way through so that you can work with your group, and complete your studies, without feeling that you have 'sold out'. Above all, avoid being drawn into arguments or situations which do not concern you. People are often happy for the non-conformist to become involved if this means that 'the blame' can be laid at her/his door.

One way of dealing with being the group member who 'sees things differently' is to try really hard to understand how others see them. As Gatrell and Turnbull (2003: 64) suggest:

You may feel you know where the boundaries should lie – but where does everyone else think they are? Understanding this might go a long way towards helping you turn conflict into a valuable chance for reflection – for yourself, if not for the rest of the group.

Additionally, or alternatively, you might find that it is possible or helpful to you to express your views through your written assignments. If you choose to tackle things in this way, you must approach the situation with care. Tutors/ supervisors and/or examiners give good marks to assignments which answer the set question, are logically and defensibly argued and draw upon relevant literature to back up arguments. An angry political statement will not meet these criteria. However, if you can work out a way in which you can make your point and *back this up* with evidence from the literature, or from your empirical research, you may be able to gain good marks *and* get your point across.

For example, a feminist student undertaking a degree in History of Art, doing an assignment on Victorian painting, might feel that the role played by women artists has been overlooked and undervalued, and that this issue has not been sufficiently highlighted in her course. It would be possible to argue this point very adeptly by drawing on the work of feminist art historians such as Deborah Cherry and Griselda Pollock. (It might be wise, though, to consult with your tutor/supervisor as you are going along to gain her/his support and advice as you develop your written work.)

Feeling 'different' because of your gender, ethnic background or appearance

It is possible to feel 'different' because you are in the minority, and this sense of difference might be experienced by you even if others in your group are welcoming and pleasant. Nirmal Puwar, in her book *Space Invaders: Bodies Out of Place*, argues that 'we are living in a moment of change' which 'disturbs the status quo' (Puwar 2004: 1). Puwar argues that, increasingly, 'women and racialized minorities' are entering organizational spaces where 'white male' professional and managerial power has previously been firmly established – such as higher education. Puwar argues that white men are the bodily 'norm' and have comfortably inhabited public spaces and positions of leadership (e.g. government, business and universities) for centuries, while 'women and racialized minorities' have historically been the 'outsiders' (Puwar 2004: 8). Puwar refers to women who occupy traditionally male and public arenas as 'space invaders' (Puwar 2004: 7); Hatt *et al.* (1999) argue that this may also be the case if you are lesbian, gay or a mother; and Woodhams and Corby (2003) argue that uninformed and unfair assumptions may also be made about you if you are disabled.

Puwar examines what happens when 'women and racialized minorities or other [minority groups] take up privileged "positions" which have not been "reserved" for them, for which they are not, in short, the somatic norm' (Puwar 2004: 1). It is notable that very few women attended university before the Second World War, and even in 1970, in the UK, there were twice as many male as female students (Hatt *et al.* 1999: 15). Although this imbalance has changed in women's favour, and there are now more women than men entering higher education in the UK, in terms of faculty, universities remain principally white, male domains with less than 20% of professorial roles held by women.

Puwar acknowledges that in policy terms the concept of 'diversity' is an important part of government and organizational policy and has 'overwhelmingly come to mean the inclusion of different bodies' (Puwar 2004: 1). Nevertheless, she argues that while women and racialized minorities may be allowed entry to spaces from which they were previously excluded (such as universities), they may still experience difficulties. Puwar examines the issues faced by those who are female, or black, or both, in the political arena and suggests that they may be faced with a sense that they do not 'belong'. She describes the experiences of British MP Tony Banks, on entering the House of Commons with Diane Abbott, a black, female MP. Tony Banks recalled:

[The smoking room] is like one of those leather enrobed clubs in Pall Mall. I took Diane Abbott in there soon after she was elected and the response from the habitués was electrifying. They didn't need to say a word. Both Diane and I knew the question (in other words what was she doing here?). But she wasn't a cleaner.

(Tony Banks 1996, quoted in Puwar 2004: 40)

Equal opportunities policies

Most universities will have equal opportunities or diversity policies in place. Nevertheless, the sense that you are part of an institution where, historically, others like you would have been excluded, may make you acutely aware of your differences. Puwar (2004: 154–5) acknowledges that it can be difficult to know what to do in these circumstances – there is no easy 'answer', and the decision about whether you work to 'fit in' with others in your group, or whether you intend to be political about your situation, may be complex. Puwar warns that

Those outsiders who do not discuss their differences and just try to blend in with the norm are more likely to be accepted and to succeed. As a strategy of survival they might judge it more pragmatic to remain silent and concentrate on the job [or assignment/research project] . . . those who are considered too vocal on gender issues may be labelled as boisterous, aggressive and hysterical . . . [and] those who choose to come out and speak against racism amongst their ranks risk being seen as engaged in renegade acts. Divulging the secrets of your own occupational tribe is a risky business indeed, especially when your 'space invader' status already marks you out and grants you a tenuous location.

(Puwar 2004: 154–5)

Whatever stance you take, it is important to remember that most institutions will have in place policies for dealing with bullying, harassment and/or discrimination, and most will publish Equal Opportunities policies in handbooks, or on their website. For example, the Open University states:

> We are committed to promoting a culture which encourages equality and diversity. We aim to be a truly inclusive organization where individual differences are respected and valued and where everyone is able to achieve their potential. Our commitment goes beyond simply following legislation. We expect all our members to support and promote our equal opportunity and diversity policy. We are proud to be a multicultural community and are determined to make sure we continue to:
>
> • treat everyone fairly with dignity and respect;
> • provide opportunities that are open to all;
> • recognize that people with different background, skills, attitudes and experiences bring fresh ideas which enrich the experience of all those who take part in the life and work of the University.
>
> (Open University 2004b: 92)

If, therefore, you feel that your experiences of feeling different have gone beyond a general sense that you do not quite 'fit in' with the rest of your group, but are related to specific instances where you feel that you are experiencing harassment due to your gender, disability, ethnic background or sexual orientation, then this might be the moment to talk to your course tutor/supervisor or student union (if you feel comfortable doing this) and/or to consult the anti-bullying and harassment policies established within your organization. (See also the section on harassment in this book on pages 146–7.)

Working in groups: summary of key points

• Many students find group work challenging, particularly if they have been 'thrown together' by faculty to work together on case studies or assignments over a lengthy period.
• Working together and sharing ideas can be beneficial to all – and you can still complete tasks successfully even if you do not all like one another.
• Try to get your group to talk things through when there are difficulties – agreeing some boundaries, and a fair share of workloads can help reduce tensions.
• Taking actions as problems arise is probably better than hoping they will just vanish.
• If you are very unhappy in your group, try to deal with problems earlier

rather than later, so that you can settle down and enjoy the course. Sometimes it is appropriate to involve faculty.

- If your views are very different from those of other group or class members, they and you might have to accept this – but you can be firm about refusing the blame for 'general' group issues, and you can try to understand the viewpoints of others.
- No student should experience discrimination on grounds of race, gender, disability or sexual orientation. Most institutions will have published policies on Equal Opportunities and Diversity.

3

Practical tips for writing assignments, dissertations and theses

Academic writing for assignments • Writing your assignment • Writing assignments: summary of key points • Writing a dissertation, or thesis • Choosing a topic • Starting to write – right from the word 'go' • Establishing a study routine • On being a 'completer/finisher': knowing when you have done enough • Concluding section and references • Writing a dissertation or thesis: summary of key points

I have already noted that this book is not a 'crammer', or a study guide in the traditional sense. This is because there are many books already available, offering specific advice on assignment writing: choosing a topic, structuring your work properly, citing references accurately, doing your dissertation and so on. However, there are some key skills which, as a part-time student, can improve both your general experience of study *and* the level of marks you will receive, at relatively little cost to yourself. The first (and arguably the most important of these) has been dealt with in the previous chapter: being well organized with your work, planning your work in advance and not leaving everything until the last minute. In this chapter, however, some further suggestions are provided which can make all the difference to the outcome – especially if you are studying part-time. These all relate to improving your writing and study skills and three aspects of part-time study – assignment writing, dissertation or project writing, and the writing of a thesis for research – are covered.

Academic writing for assignments

It is important to think about what is meant by 'academic writing', and what this means for *you*. It has been argued that academic institutions are often firmly focused on the subject they are teaching, but without explicitly teaching the academic literacy skills required (Curry 2003). This is seen as an omission on the part of universities, especially in the context of the push for widening participation in higher education, meaning that, if students are drawn from diverse backgrounds, those who have less understanding of the communicative demands of the academy may be unfairly disadvantaged (Curry 2003). In addition, reading and writing at university is infused by the cultural context of particular disciplines, so that as well as learning the craft of writing for academic purposes, students are also required to accommodate the expectations of their own subject area (Richardson 2004). Such expectations may be even more problematic for part-time students than they are for full-timers. Students who are around campus may be able to 'pick up' the language and the cultural context of their discipline far more easily than those who are only there in person for short periods – or, if studying at a distance, not at all.

Whatever the expectations within your discipline, there are still some general guidelines which could be useful – no matter what your subject. Assignments are commonly associated with undergraduate study, but quite often masters students and PhD students are required to produce them in the early stages of their courses, so this section should be relevant for students working at all levels. Let's suppose you have completed the reading and other work involved in your first module and your first assignment is now due. One helpful way of starting – before beginning to think about what should (and what should not) go into an assignment – is to consider the purpose of assignments.

The purpose of assignments

Giles and Hedge (2002: 111–12) offer the following four suggestions:

- To reinforce and consolidate learning.
- To evaluate learning.
- To demonstrate knowledge and understanding.
- To apply theoretical concepts to the 'real' world.

For students beginning a masters or a research degree, or undergraduates for whom a dissertation is a course requirement, I would suggest a fifth and additional purpose. Assignments are a useful starting point. They get you going, boost your confidence and help you lay the groundwork for your dissertation or thesis. So a fifth purpose might be

• To help you get started and lay the foundations for a dissertation or thesis.

I will consider the five main purposes of assignments one by one, basing the first four suggestions on the suggestions of Giles and Hedge (2002):

To reinforce and consolidate learning

Giles and Hedge (2002: 111) argue that 'writing forces you to consider what you have been learning'. They suggest that the discipline of having to write things down helps you remember and internalize what you have learned. They also point out that writing about what you have learned can help you identify, for yourself, anything that you have not fully understood. Being forced to write about something in an assignment gives you the chance to revisit difficult concepts and clarify these for yourself.

To evaluate learning

The second purpose of assignments is to allow your tutor/supervisor to evaluate your understanding in relation to what has been taught on your course. How well have you understood what has been taught and how effectively can you apply this? Are there any gaps in your knowledge or understanding? As Giles and Hedge point out, it is important not to feel intimidated by the evaluation process. Your assignment will usually be returned to you with feedback, as well as with a grade, and you can draw upon the learning from each assignment so as to improve the next one. Giles and Hedge (2002: 111) make the very valid point: 'I'd prefer a tutor/supervisor to read an assignment and tell me I'd misunderstood something before I had to . . . write an examination . . . Assignments are useful progress indicators for your tutor/supervisor *and* for you.'

To demonstrate knowledge and understanding

Your assignment gives you the chance to show the examiner, your tutor/supervisor, and to prove to *yourself*, what you can do. In your assignments you can provide evidence that you have read the course texts and understood the relevant concepts and theories. The more assignments you write, the easier this will become. Writing assignments gives you the chance to improve your skills at communicating your arguments and getting your point across in a given number of words and to a given topic. In writing your assignment, you might find that you sharpen up your own logic and argument and that this will give you increased confidence when presenting your point of view to others. For those readers who are employed, or seeking employment, enhancing your abilities to explain things (and sometimes to argue your case) might prove very useful at work.

To apply theoretical concepts to the 'real' world

Giles and Hedge are writing particularly with managers in mind. They argue that, for management students, the application of course concepts to workplace practices and experiences is essential so that students can see for themselves the relevance of what they have studied to the worlds in which they work. While many of those reading this book will be studying subjects other than management, the chance to apply, or at least to consider, what has been learned in the context of workplace practices will be invaluable to many who are studying vocationally based subjects. The application of learning to practice may even be a required course element for those taking skills-based courses such as Childhood and Youth Studies, Social Work or Information Technology and Computing.

To help you get started and lay the foundations for your dissertation or thesis

It is not unusual for masters courses or research degrees to begin with a taught element, in which you lay the foundations for your project or thesis. Even if you are doing a PhD, your tutor/supervisor or course convenor might set assignments in the first year. The experience of doing assignments – even if you are starting a higher degree, having just completed an undergraduate or a masters course – will help you begin what might be quite a daunting piece of work (in the case of a PhD, possibly up to 100,000 words) with a manageable piece of writing. Students undertaking higher degrees who are doing coursework can save time by bearing in mind the ultimate goal at each stage. Assignments can be used not only to ensure that you have laid the academic foundations for what will follow, but as stepping stones on the way to producing a thesis or dissertation. You might want to ask yourself questions as you progress through each assignment, considering how far it might be relevant to your dissertation or thesis.

Relating assignment writing to your forthcoming thesis/dissertation – questions to ask yourself as you go along

At each stage, the experience of assignment writing gives you the chance to think:

- Am I sufficiently interested in this topic to want to follow it up in a dissertation/thesis?
- Is there more to say than I can write in one assignment, and would this therefore be a suitable subject for further research in my dissertation/thesis?

- Do my marks suggest that I would do well if I chose this topic for my dissertation/thesis?

Find out what is expected of you

Having considered the purpose of assignment writing, there is one more preparatory step worth taking *before* you begin writing, which will stand you in good stead throughout your programme. This is to find out, and be sure that you are clear about, what is expected of you at each stage of your course. Understanding what is required of you at the beginning of a programme can be difficult, especially for part-time students, who dip in and out of university life and might find it hard to pick things up as they go along. But there are some things which you need to know, and which – if they are not stated in your course handbook or website – it is reasonable to ask your tutor/supervisor at the outset. For example, is all your reading provided for you by the university/college? Or are you supposed to do your own literature searches and read widely beyond the set texts? If you are supposed to be on a flexible learning programme (handing in assignments when you are ready), how flexible is 'flexible'? Can you really take your own time, or do you need to produce a minimum amount of work each year to stay on your programme? Read your course handbook carefully, and try and clarify for yourself, at the outset, what the basic requirements are for you to remain on, and succeed in, your course.

Writing your assignment

I will assume that you have started your course and you are now ready to take the plunge and write your first assignment. This will be more daunting for some students than for others. If you have recently completed an undergraduate course, then although the word length and standard might be revised upwards for a higher degree, the basic requirement of pulling together your learning, and producing a piece of written work, will seem less daunting than if you have never done a degree or if you are a mature student who has not been involved in academic study for many years. There are many study texts available which offer help with assignment writing, and probably some which relate specifically to your own topic area. Additionally, it is appreciated that your assignments may be set in various forms, partly depending on the nature of your course, and could include case studies and numeric, psychological, work-based or scientific exercises. However, as Talbot (2003: 94) suggests, it is often the writing of traditional, essay-style assignments 'that creates most anxiety amongst students'. In what follows, therefore, I shall not attempt to cover everything in detail, but to suggest some basic strategies which might help you tackle the task you have been set, and might also save you valuable time.

Read the instructions and proceed with care

Giles and Hedge (2002: 112) get straight to the point and state that:

> first and foremost, a good assignment answers the question. It's no good writing an excellent answer to a question that wasn't set, or writing an answer to only part of the question. Straying from the point, however interesting and well written, will [not earn you good marks]. You must, therefore, take time to analyse the question. Read and re-read it and at every stage in your assignment go back to remind yourself of the precise wording of the question.

So: begin by reading your question carefully. Make sure you have understood exactly what is required of you before you start. Take note of what is said about the word limit and check whether the question has more than one part. If it does, ensure that you answer all aspects of it, not just those bits that you find easiest, or most interesting (remember the tutor/supervisor or examiner is using the assignment as a tool to evaluate your knowledge of the subject). Think carefully about what you are being asked to do. This is unlikely to involve simply describing what you have read in textbooks or online. You will probably be required to *analyse* your material in some way, producing some definitions and providing some analysis in the context of your taught materials. You will be expected to explain and defend your decisions at each point, in the context of your course material. Do not be tempted to stray off the point. You must stick to what you have been asked to do. This is because, as well as seeking to find out how *much* you know, the person marking your paper will wish to see how well you can *apply* what you know to the question asked. The marker will also be looking at whether you can achieve this within your word limit, and how far you can make sensible decisions about what is relevant material, and what can be left out. Going over your word limit is risky, and may result in loss of marks, as Scott Holtham (2000: 75) discovered:

> [My assignment] was only supposed to be 1500 words but . . . I fell into the trap of convincing myself that it was impossible to address the issue in fewer than 2000 words. My paper was returned thoroughly annotated and I was flattered to receive a mark just under distinction. I was penalised for excessive length – a salutary lesson in the necessity of getting to the point.

Planning your assignment

Imagine, for example, that you were doing a degree in History of Art. It is appreciated that this might be a bit of a stretch for students doing a science degree, but using this example will help me make the points about being analytical and relevant in your answer.

Your assignment question might ask:

Using course texts as a starting point, evaluate the impact of the Pre-Raphaelites on the Victorian art scene up to and including 1856 (word limit 2000)

The Pre-Raphaelites were a group of young, male British painters who formed a 'brotherhood' in 1848. Their work was considered to be controversial and unconventional, and at the same time they attracted many followers.

Before you started work on this assignment, you would need to decide what, or who, to include, and what to leave out. This would mean thinking about exactly which artists you are going to include in the category 'Pre-Raphaelite' before you begin. Should you include only the three artists who were the founder members of the Pre-Raphaelite Brotherhood (Millais, Rossetti and Holman Hunt), or should you also include various of their followers? Should you consider the work of individual Pre-Raphaelites before the group started, or are you supposed to focus only on the short period from 1848 when these artists were working together?

You could begin by explaining to the reader of your assignment how you have defined 'Pre-Raphaelite', and how and why you have made your decision. The set question provides you with a 'clue' about how you might make this decision. Since you are asked to focus on 'course texts', you could reasonably expect to find some clues about how you define the parameters of your assignment in the books on your reading list.

You would also need to think about how to define the 'Victorian art scene'. You might decide that this should include the exhibitions held at London's Royal Academy and the writings of art critic John Ruskin, especially if the Royal Academy and Ruskin were discussed in your course texts.

The request that you 'evaluate' the impact of the Pre-Raphaelites suggests that you need to do more than merely list or describe events. In this case you will be expected not only to provide a history of what happened, but also to appraise, or make a judgement, on the impact of the Pre-Raphaelites on the 'Victorian art scene'. In making your evaluation, you will need to be sure to defend your position in the context of the course texts upon which you have been asked to draw. You will also need to ensure that, in making your appraisal, you have considered both sides of the argument – and you need to give your reasons for coming down in favour of one side rather than the other. Thus, you might wish to support the view of art critic John Ruskin that the Pre-Raphaelites brought a breath of much needed fresh air to the Victorian art scene, but you would need to have already explained why other critics and painters were unimpressed with what the Pre-Raphaelites were doing. A detailed consideration of your assignment question should provide you with a sense of what the focus of your assignment should be. If you are uncertain, this would be the moment to consult your tutor/supervisor, who will probably appreciate the fact that you have already made an effort to understand what is required.

How much do you need to read for an assignment? The assignment question discussed above, which suggests the course texts should be a 'starting point' only, gives a hint that you will need to read more than just the essential texts on your reading list – especially if you seek high marks. While you can't possibly read everything that has ever been written on your subject, and although you will probably have been given a reading list, course tutors/ supervisors will encourage you to read more widely than the course texts. Once you have worked out what your assignment question is seeking, you are in a good position to write an assignment plan. This should be specific. You need to decide how many sections there will be, what will go in each section, and how many words will be allocated to each section. Once you have completed this task, it will be easier to be selective about what you read. Elizabeth, below, explains how she structured her assignments carefully and thought through in advance how many words she would need for each section. This enabled her to write an appropriate amount at the outset, and she was not obliged to waste precious time trying to cut down sections (or whole assignments) that were too long.

Student experience

The thing that helped me the most was learning to structure my assignments. This meant that the first thing I did was to organize the word count into the appropriate sections. So if I was writing 1500 words, I might do something like this: introduction 200, literature 500, main body of discussion 500, conclusions 300, and so on.

I always headed up my draft with the assignment question too so that I didn't lose sight of what they were asking for. I always began my draft assignment with the phrase 'The purpose of this assignment is to . . . In particular it . . . It does this by . . .'. I changed these once I had completed the assignment but it really helped focus me. The other element that helped was signposting, i.e. informing the reader what I was doing with the structure or argument. So an example might be: 'Having covered the main elements of the law, I now turn to X', or 'This raises questions about a, b and c. It is to these questions that I now turn.'

I know this might sound a bit pedantic, but I think it was probably useful for the reader so they knew what to expect and where I was heading. It was also helpful to me, as it saved time because I was clear about what I intended to write at the start of each section.

(Elizabeth, postgraduate diploma in Educational Psychology)

Ensure that your work is presented in the correct style

Your faculty will have rules and regulations about how your work should be presented and handed in. Make sure that you follow these closely. If your faculty asks for work to be double spaced, presented in a ring binder and handed in in triplicate, make sure that your assignments fulfil these requirements exactly. There may be good reasons for setting the rules as they are, and you want to create a good impression at the outset. Everything should be neatly set out as directed in the course instructions. If you are allowed to e-mail your assignments to your faculty, make sure that your files are presented in such a way that they are easy to print out and get into order. If at all possible, send in hard copy – even if this has to be sent at some expense. This is because you are then sure that your work reaches the examiner *in the correct format*, and you are not reliant on others to ensure that pages are printed out and collated in the right order. It is also easy to see – if you print out your work yourself – that you have submitted the correct, and most recent, version. There is no question, then, that you might have submitted an outdated version of a document without even realizing this, or a document from which a whole section might be missing because pages were not put together in the right order. There is no substitute for taking responsibility for printing out and presenting your own work, so try and manage your work yourself from beginning to end.

Referencing

You will be expected, as you discuss the work of others within your assignment, to acknowledge all the other texts, writings or other sources from which you have drawn. This is not only courteous (you are recognizing how others' ideas have influenced your work) but essential. If you do not reference your sources, you may be accused of plagiarism, an 'offence' which universities take very seriously. The topics of referencing and plagiarism are issues which worry many students (whether they are writing an undergraduate assignment or a PhD thesis). In my view, the problem of plagiarism may be more of a worry for students who are not on campus full-time because part-timers may not have access to the same networks, or be around to pick up 'tips' about how to avoid plagiarism in the same way that full-timers are. For this reason, I will devote a complete section to plagiarism and referencing (which includes a section on protecting your own work) in Chapter 4.

Allow time to read through and edit at the end

Thinking back to my own experience as a part-time MBA student, I remember fellow students who were so pressured and disorganized that they were completing and printing out essays at 5.00 am on the due date. As well as putting you under extreme stress, this leaves no time to correct mistakes and can result in 'howlers', for example the names of key authors, or political figures, misspelled throughout. In more recent years, one group of students, undertaking a course on the history of social science, were supposed to have a good understanding of the work of two famous writers on human behaviour: Max Weber and Jeremy Bentham. In his report, the examiner deduced a link between misspellings and those students who had drawn upon very little other than their own lecture notes. In one particular assignment, he observed references to 'Webber' and 'Benthom' and judged that this might indicate a lack of familiarity with the work of the writers in question!

Even if you have spent the minimum amount of time answering your assignment question, you might make up some lost ground by allowing enough time to check things through at the end. Items to concentrate on are spellings, presentation and mathematical calculations. If you are including tables or diagrams to illustrate your point, even if your course is science- or mathematics-based, *you must ensure that these are neatly set out and carefully numbered.* You must refer to them in the text so that the reader is clear *why you have included them and what they are supposed to show.* Ironically, it is often those students who are on the 'borderline' who fail to read through and edit at the end of their assignments, even though these are the group whose work would most benefit from a thorough check through before submission, meaning that some marks which would otherwise be lost through careless mistakes might be clawed back. First impressions count – even to academic markers and examiners – and while you cannot pull the wool over their eyes entirely (if you haven't done any work they will know), they are more likely to be well disposed to neat, well-presented work which reads well, with each section properly headed and numbered.

Make the most of feedback

It is often difficult to appreciate and apply feedback on assignments. This is partly because marking may take several weeks and you may be well into your next task by the time you receive feedback on the previous one. Thus, you have rather lost interest in what went before, so making a note of the mark and feeling a sense of relief when grades are good often supersedes the desire to read feedback. Students may also skim through the written comments because the whole process of marking and providing feedback can be painful for the recipient. Nevertheless, it is important that you do read the feedback. As I observed earlier, the purpose of setting assignments is so that course tutors/supervisors and examiners can evaluate your progress on the course. As Talbot (2003: 101) observes (and as Imogen describes, below), good feedback 'will help you see how to improve your work and it will help you recognise where and how to make your argument more clearly'.

Student experience

Throughout the course my marks went up, down and up. And what kept me going was my own determination, the tutorials, reading and the freedom to think which came from that. It has to be said, it wasn't always easy to hear the feedback about assignments and it was more difficult still to take it on board. But I suppose essentially, what made the difference and made me keep going was that writing the assignments enabled me to recapture my professional passion, and also being supported and validated by the academic staff, who acknowledged that my ideas could have academic value, was motivating. In a practical sense, the feedback I received on my written work helped me to structure my ideas and to focus my reading and analytical resources.

(Imogen, part-time masters, Political Science)

Writing assignments: summary of key points

- The main purposes of assignments are to evaluate and consolidate your learning, to show that you have understood course concepts and to lay the foundations for a bigger piece of work.
- Find out what is expected of you, and ensure that what you write addresses the question that you have been asked.
- Ensure that your work is presented in the correct style, and that your references are accurate, neat and tidy.
- Allow plenty of time for reading through and editing at the end.
- Make the most of feedback and use this to improve your skills on each occasion.

Writing a dissertation, or thesis

There are many helpful books and papers on thesis writing. For this reason (and since I can only include a limited amount of information in this general text) I shall give a brief overview of some of the best. In my view, two of the most valuable books on thesis writing are Murray (2002) *How to Write a Thesis* and Flowerdew and Martin (2005) *Methods in Human Geography: A Guide for Students Doing a Research Project*. It should be noted that although Flowerdew and Martin are writing for geography students, their book provides excellent and straightforward advice for *any* student writing a thesis or dissertation. Whether you are an engineering student, a psychologist or an historian,

Methods in Human Geography will assist in covering the whole process of thesis writing, including choosing a topic, researching and reviewing what others have written on your topic, choosing an appropriate methodology and producing the written thesis. If you are undertaking a work-based research project, you may find Gatrell and Turnbull (2003) useful. Although the title *Your MBA with Distinction: Developing a Systematic Approach to Succeeding in your Business Degree* suggests that the principal readers of the book should be MBA students, Gatrell and Turnbull provide helpful advice on applying theory to 'real-world' problems and useful sections on dissertation and assignment writing, which would be useful to any student whose part-time study relates to their paid work. Jennifer Mason (2002) offers help to those trying to narrow down their research question. Although her book is written for qualitative researchers, her suggestions are also helpful to those doing quantitative work. And Saunders *et al.* (2000), in their book *Research Methods for Business Students*, provide an excellent guide to the range of methods relevant and available to all (not just business students), as well as offering sensible advice about which approach you might use for which research problem. Sanders *et al.* also offer a 'steer' about how you might manage your ethical concerns, which you will need to address if you are doing empirical research which depends on human subjects.

Given the wide range of books which offer advice on thesis writing, it is not intended to try and summarize, here, everything that has ever been written! There are, however, three topics which cause anxieties for all students, but which I think are particularly relevant to those studying part-time. These are: getting started – choosing and defining a topic; beginning to write (and keeping going); and finishing off.

Choosing a topic

Choosing a topic is challenging for all students, but in my view is more tricky for part-time students than for others (regardless of the academic level at which part-time students are studying). This is because they may be studying in relative isolation from their institution, and the opportunities for bouncing ideas around with others may be limited. This is the time – probably more than any other during your programme – when you need to be able to share ideas with other students. If you are studying at a distance, and have not previously made use of online discussion groups, now is the time to do so.

For part-time students the choice of topic may be made more difficult by their distance from their institution. Of course, you might choose to expand upon something that you wrote as an assignment, or heard in a lecture (as could a full-time student). However, being part-time might narrow your options because, by studying at a distance or 'off-campus' you may feel isolated from the 'buzz' of what is going on. What are people talking about, and writing about at the moment? What are the key academic issues of the day, and who is working on them? One way of following this up might be through undertaking specific searches on the internet for what is happening in your field. This might give you a general sense of what is being discussed in the media, for example, but it might also help to look at what has been happening at conferences in your field, and this might give you an idea of what is current.

A sociology student interested in doing some work on family practices might, therefore, look at what is happening on the British Sociological Association website. Are there any forthcoming or previous conferences in your topic area? What issues were/are to be covered in the papers presented, and who will present them? Have the presenters written anything that you could read, to see if the subject might be appropriate for you to study? The student seeking to do research on family practices, looking at the issues addressed at the British Sociological Association (BSA) Conference for 2006, would observe that there were papers and discussions on single-sex marriages, infidelity within marriage, and single fatherhood, all of which are topical and might provide ideas for research. A further trawl around the website could spark off some interesting ideas for criminologists, or those interested in the sociology of work. In 2006 Teela Sanders' book *Sex Work: A Risky Business* was nominated for the Philip Abrams Memorial Prize and is one of a growing number of texts and papers on crime, policy and sex industries. For those interested in the sociology of technology, or the idea of living in a 'surveillance society', the subject matter of the 2007 BSA conference – identities, technologies and relationships – might get you thinking.

Feasibility

At whatever level, it is important to ensure that your chosen topic is feasible. If your work is to be library or text-based, you need to ensure that the literature to which you need access is available before you start, especially if you are investigating 'primary' sources. For example, if you were an historian looking at newsletters from a Scottish country parish in the 1950s, you would need to know whether these were available in the local library or records office, and whether you would be allowed to access them. If they were kept in a church, would you be allowed to borrow them? Or would you be expected to sit and read them on site? And how would this fit in with your other work/family arrangements? If you aim to write a thesis on family histories, or social trends in education, it may well be that you can access much of the material you need via the internet. However, you need to ascertain whether this will be at no cost (either because it is free to all, or because your institution already pays a subscription), or whether you will be required to pay a fee to gain access to the information you need. Some genealogical and/or statistical information is only available if you pay for it.

If you are expected to undertake an empirical, work-based or 'outdoor' study, then you need to think through carefully what you would need to do, or who you would need to talk to for your research, before you settle on your topic. This is even more crucial for part-time students than it is for full-timers. Since your time is likely to be limited, the discovery that you will have to change tack, or topic, part way through your study might seriously constrain your chances of completing your research. It is worth establishing the practicalities of what you will need at the outset. Can you access the data you need? For instance, an environmental scientist wishing to look at the coastline in Cornwall might require access to privately owned land. In such a case, it would be important to ensure that this would be possible before embarking on the study.

If you are doing a study about human behaviour, are there any procedures you need to follow before you can start, and how much time will these take before you can get going? (For example, any study involving school children will need the permission both of the school and of the parents.) Once you have laid the ground work, are you sure that you can gain the information you need from the individuals you are targeting? It is worth considering a pilot study at an early stage to test out the practicality of your research design. For example, one group of students seeking to investigate how the market for funerals might be expanded found that their idea of doing an online survey was a 'non-starter'. Most respondents did not want to think about their own funeral in advance of the event, and therefore almost nobody got beyond the first question, which was:

Have you given any thought to the kind of funeral you would like?
YES/NO

Researching within your own organization

Some students studying human behaviour will be doing employment, or practice-based research, possibly within their own organization. This is much more likely to be the case if you are part-time than if you are full-time. Full-time students may be parachuted into an organization to do an internship or 'placement' which will involve a thesis, or research project. While they may hope that their placement will result in employment when they have finished their course of study, they also have the option of moving on. One student of mine, whom I shall call Betty, undertook a brave and highly political critique of the marketing strategy espoused by 'Central Training', the organization in which she was 'placed' for five months. As it turned out, the organization accepted her recommendations and offered her a permanent post at the end of her degree. They accepted her criticisms that their existing strategy was narrow and old-fashioned and involved her in developing new ways of marketing their product. Had the outcome been different, however (i.e. she received good marks for her dissertation, but found the organization to be unreceptive to – or even offended by – her observations), she could simply have applied for a job elsewhere. She need never have contacted Central Training again.

For part-time students, the situation is often very different. Many part-time degree programmes are designed specifically to allow you to do fieldwork and research within your own field and/or organization. This can be advantageous – it affords you the opportunity to directly apply to practice the theoretical concepts that you are studying. This helps you to internalize your learning and also to 'try out' different approaches in the most practical sense. This opportunity also, however, comes with some risks attached. You may be seeking information from individuals within organizations where you are well known, or, indeed, employed. You might be talking to people whom you manage, or who manage you. They might want to read what you have written, and your recommendations might (like Betty's) have implications for organizational policies.

If this sounds like your situation, you will need to think carefully about the politics of what you are proposing to do. Are you choosing a topic which might be particularly sensitive? In Betty's case, for example, staff in the marketing and sales department were bound to be affected by the updated policies and practices which she was recommending. And have you discussed your proposed topic fully with your line manager? It might be worth trying to obtain her/his agreement to your topic in writing – you don't want your research to limit your career. Additionally – especially if you are doing PhD research over a long period – you might want to think through how you/your research will be affected if you become disenchanted with your paid work (see Paul's experience below).

Student experience

One of the advantages of part-time study when it's going well is that it energizes work and vice versa. However, researching your own organization when you are feeling out of sorts with your employer can be tough. I experienced quite a difficult year when I was at a turning point in my research (which was about my organization) and I was also finding work quite stressful. This meant that everything – paid work and study – was infused with a sense of frustration, of not making the progress I sought to achieve. Then I sort of came to terms with what was happening at work and thought 'Oh well' – no point in letting this take over my life; I may as well just get on with things and see what happens. I am much more relaxed about my paid work now, and this has had a hugely beneficial effect on my thesis. I have produced more in the last three or four months than I did in the previous twelve. Having a supervisor who understands part-time study issues is especially helpful in this regard. I can't tell her how hard it all is because she knows – she has done it herself. I respond to being encouraged in a no-nonsense way!

(Paul, part-time PhD, Religious Studies)

Scoping your topic

Finally, the scope and breadth of your topic needs to be in keeping with the kind of thesis you are doing. In an undergraduate dissertation of, say, 10–15,000 words, you might have the time and the capacity to review some important literature on the criminalization of female sex work, but it is unlikely that you would be able to create the opportunity to undertake an empirical study. At PhD level, students in criminology would have more flexibility. Assuming that they had been able to negotiate access to their study group at a reasonably early stage (by, say, the end of the first year), they might be able to undertake research on crime and sex work which involved doing empirical work with women involved in the sex industry.

Is your topic interesting?

The warnings about topic feasibility are not intended to be off-putting or to stifle inventiveness, or ambition, but are included here merely to try and avoid 'false starts' which can waste precious time at the beginning. The discussion about thesis topics and feasibility leads me to the issue of whether your topic is interesting to you. In my view, feeling that what you are doing is interesting is essential for all students, but even more so for part-timers. The higher the level at which you are studying, and the longer your thesis, the more important it is that your topic 'burns you up'. For part-time PhD students, who will be required to sustain interest in what they are doing for around five or six years, maybe more, the idea of burning the midnight oil in order to pursue a sensible but uninspiring subject does not seem realistic. Your research topic should be like a good novel – impossible to put down.

Does your topic provide you with a research question, or problem?

This can be a tricky question to answer at the early stages, but, as Gatrell and Flowerdew (2005: 43) observe, it is important that you settle on a topic that poses:

> a research problem: a question, or set of questions that are worth asking, an issue that merits attention or requires solving. Probably the main criterion [for judging whether your project is deemed to be 'research'] is originality. Do not imagine that this means coming up with an entirely novel theory or completely new idea, but it does mean avoiding the application of old methods to old problems, or the umpteenth replication of an idea that might have been fashionable thirty years ago.

It is important that your research question is relevant, and that you can relate it either to what has already been written in your field, or to policy, or workplace practices. As you are developing your research ideas, you might ask yourself the question: 'To whom would my research be interesting, and relevant, other than me?'

It is worth noting, here, that the need to produce a thesis which is 'original' is even more important for PhD students than it is for undergraduates or masters students. PhD students are required to make an original contribution to academic knowledge, and their work must be of a standard appropriate for publication in scholarly journals. It can be harder for part-time PhD students, who may not be as much in the 'swing' of what is going on in their academic department as are full-time students, to shape and define a topic which is original. For this reason – and because the concept of 'originality' is complex for all, but so *very* important if you are a PhD student – a separate section on 'originality' is included in the next chapter, following on from the discussion about plagiarism.

Starting to write – right from the word 'go'

One of the hardest aspects of producing a dissertation is putting the first words down on paper. Many set aside a period of time near the deadline for the work to be handed in as 'writing up time', but delaying the inevitable can often be seriously detrimental to the written product. Even when you finally sit down to the task it is amazing how many jobs become more important than putting pen to paper. That cup of coffee seems particularly tempting . . .

It is essential to begin writing early and to continue writing as the research develops.

(Boyle 2005: 304, my emphasis)

Murray (2002) and Delamont *et al.* (1997) underline the importance of writing 'little and often' (Murray 2002), right from the outset. The more you can get into the habit of writing, the less daunting it becomes. Delamont *et al.* suggest that all writers can benefit from following two 'golden rules' which are:

1 Write early and often.
2 Don't get it right, get it written.

These writers argue that 'writing early and often' is important because:

• The more you write, the easier it gets.
• If you write every day, it becomes a habit.

- Tiny bits of writing add up to a lot of writing. Break the writing up into small bits. If you write 100 words on X, 200 words on Y . . . it all mounts up.
- The longer you leave it unwritten the worse the task becomes.

(Adapted from Delamont *et al.* 1997: 121)

The 'don't get it right, get it written' rule works because:

- Until it is on paper, no one can help you get it right. You can show your draft [to your tutor/supervisor] who can advise you.
- Drafting is a vital stage in clarifying thought.
- Drafting reveals the places where you need to do further work – which you cannot identify until your ideas are written down.

(Adapted from Delamont *et al.* 1997: 121)

Even if you do have a 'chunk' of time available in which to write, it is sensible to

'think about writing projects, including . . . theses, in terms of sensible and manageable chunks of effort . . . Sensible planning and regular work habits can help to transform writing into perfectly manageable everyday activities.

(Delamont *et al.* 1997: 126)

Like Delamont *et al.*, Murray (2002) recognizes that it can be very difficult to 'approach writing "cold" ' (Delamont *et al.* 1997: 127). In the context of her advice that you should aim to become a 'serial writer', Murray offers helpful strategies to enable you to begin to write regularly, in short bursts. Murray (2002: 79–80) suggests beginning your writing with a 'warm-up exercise' to get you started. She recommends beginning each writing session by writing for no more than five minutes to simple 'prompts', which might go along the lines of:

- What did I write about last time?
- What am I going to write about today?

The idea of a 'prompt' is a useful tip which will help you get started. It will also provide you with the beginnings of a writing agenda, enabling you to make the most of the time you have available to you which, as a part-time student, might be very limited. Paul Boyle (2005) advises that you should plan the process of writing each section in advance and that your plan should be flexible enough so that you can adapt, and include new or unexpected findings as you go along.

Establishing a study routine

Once you get going, it is essential to establish a routine. Most experts on academic writing make the point that it is crucial to establish a routine and to write little and often, in order to make the task of putting pen to paper (or finger to keyboard) seem like a habit rather than a rare and mountainous event (Delamont *et al.* 1997; Murray 2002; Gatrell and Turnbull 2003; Boyle 2005). Routine has been the key to successful writing by some of the world's greatest and best known writers. The French novelist Georges Simenon was incredibly prolific and produced close to 400 novels during his lifetime, as well as newspaper articles, stories and autobiographical books (Assouline 1997). However, Simenon had the luxury of devoting all his time to his writing – he was not attempting to hold down a 'day job', or undertake demanding duties as a carer over long periods. Simenon writes of his routine:

> My existence is divided into periods of fifteen days. In each period I compose one novel . . . I type my books myself, directly, without writing them out by hand first. No touch ups or modifications . . . My books generally have twelve chapters. I compose one chapter each morning, no more . . . That's twelve chapters, twelve days, plus the preparation day for a total of thirteen. On the fourteenth day I read the manuscript, correcting typographical errors, punctuation. Then I take the text to my publisher. On the fifteenth day I have friends over, answer letters I've received during the past two weeks . . . Then it all begins again, exactly the same way for the next fifteen days.
>
> (Simenon, quoted in Assouline 1997: 102)

The idea of establishing a study routine is, arguably, more important for part-time students than it is for full-time students. This is because full-timers are usually based in the same location, and are probably working in groups, either informally or as part of their course. For these students, routines will probably emerge naturally – attending a seminar followed by coffee and a visit to the library, or living in shared accommodation, sharing supper and then settling down to a couple of hours study. For part-time students, the idea of 'routine' may be very different. You are trying to fit study around other things in your life (such as employment!) which may at times have to take priority. It may be difficult to share any kind of routine with course colleagues because you could be located thousands of miles away from one another. If you are doing your course online, you may be operating in different time zones. Your writing routine must, therefore, be consciously defined and developed by you. It might be interesting for part-time students to consider that many famous writers, at least for part of their career, wrote only part-time and had to work out ways of managing their writing career alongside their 'day job'. The great

Russian playwright Anton Chekhov, for example, produced his written work on a part-time basis because his main career was medicine, and from time to time his job as a doctor took priority over his fictional writing. In 1891, he managed to produce a book about medical conditions in Siberia while also writing short stories, establishing a routine to keep himself 'on track':

> All through the summer of 1891 [Chekhov] worked on Mondays, Tuesdays and Wednesdays on his [Siberian] book, . . . with Sundays reserved for short stories.
>
> (Callow 1998: 167–8)

Routine means different things to different people, but at the very least, you could interpret this as finding a regular time to write, and a special place which is yours. Boyle (2005) and Murray (2002) emphasize the need to establish good study routines, which will differ from person to person:

> You are not alone if you find it difficult to begin what appears to be a daunting piece of work and it is well worth putting some time into defining your optimum writing environment. For some . . . the exact conditions may be [quite] elaborate. Usually it helps to equate a particular location, such as a particular spot in the library, with writing.
>
> (Boyle 2005: 304)

You can follow Boyle's and Murray's (2000) advice even if you are nowhere near a library, and living somewhere small with no obvious place for study. Jasmin describes her experiences of doing her law degree part-time:

Student experience

In the first house that I shared with my partner, I studied at home on Monday to Thursday evenings and went into my empty office every other Saturday afternoon. The house was not big enough for me to leave everything scattered about, so I worked at the kitchen table. So after dinner we would clear everything away so the kitchen was immaculate and he would leave me to it for a good couple of hours. I kept a big box underneath the table so that I could easily transfer my work from the box on the floor to the table, or I could put it in the car and take it to the office, without losing my place. This was not an easy situation, as I am not the tidiest of people (to say the least!). But the sense that I was in a routine – the table at night in a cleared kitchen and the quiet of the office on a Saturday sort of got me into the habit. Clear up, get box out, write! So I did manage it for nearly two years and gained my degree.

(Jasmin, undergraduate, Law)

Whether you write at home or in the library, and whether your 'best' writing time is in the morning, afternoon or evening, getting into a routine with a regular place and time in which to write can be very helpful and is more likely to produce results than if you are waiting for creative inspiration to strike.

But what if you are out of the habit of writing and have not written anything at all for a period of time? And what if you simply can't get going again? Many students experience 'writer's block' at some point in their programme, and ways of dealing with an inability to write, and how to pick up writing after a break in study are therefore discussed in the next chapter.

On being a 'completer/finisher': knowing when you have done enough

Dissertations will involve substantially more time than ordinary essays and they will contribute far more to the assessment of the final degree. Consequently, you should give special care to the writing-up procedure. The examiner has little to go on except the final product and it would be unfortunate if a careless write-up masked the good work put in to the project as a whole.

(Boyle 2005: 302)

The third aspect of thesis writing which many part-time scholars find challenging is the task of completing and submitting. Arguably, pulling everything together and finishing off is a greater challenge for part-time students than full-time students because the research and writing process has been spread over a longer period of time. It becomes more difficult to pull all the strands together and make sure that the 'end product' is coherent and polished. Apart from feeling that you 'ought' to have finished your thesis, because you are facing a deadline, how will you know when you have done enough? And how might you decide what to include in your thesis, and what to leave out?

What have you achieved?

It helps at this stage to return to your original research question. Have you done what you set out to do when you identified your research topic? If not, why not? Try to summarize for yourself, in a few sentences, what it is that you have achieved in your research. A review and critique of the literature on the criminalization of sex work? A study of parish magazines, with a view to understanding the links between village and church life in 1950s Scotland? A study of marketing strategy within a well-known consultancy firm, with recommendations for their future policy? Even if you are studying at PhD level (in which case you will need to demonstrate that you have made an identifiable contribution to academic knowledge), the step of identifying how far you have met the aims of your original research question will help you decide whether you have 'finished', or whether there is further work to do. It may be the case that you have not achieved everything you set out to do. This need not mean that you need to rush out and do more work, but it might mean that you need to consider (and discuss) the limitations of your approach.

Then look at your thesis. Have you included all the information that you need, in order to give the reader a full understanding of all the work you have done?

Boyle (2005: 303) suggests that your finished thesis should include the following six components:

- Identification/outline of the question you are trying to answer.
- Important descriptive material [about what you have read]. Even if your reader/examiner knows a great deal about your subject you must *show* that you have done the preliminary work (original emphasis).
- The manner in which you set about answering your research question, why your chosen method/technique/mode of analysis was chosen.
- The findings that you produced.
- The relevance of these findings to knowledge/practice/policy.
- The limitations of your research.

Boyle's criteria for recognizing when your work is finished are similar to those advocated by Murray (2002). Murray adds the reminder that you should pay attention to feedback from your tutor/supervisor. Does she/he think you are ready? Or is there further work to be done? It is worth listening to her/his advice. If she/he feels that something needs more attention, it is likely that your examiner might share the same view.

A final pointer for how you will know that your work is as 'complete' as it needs to be before you submit it is because you have a sense, yourself, that you are ready to tidy it up and hand it in. Ideally, this should *not* be because you are fed up, or because time is running out, but because you have taken ownership of your research. You feel you can locate and defend the 'contribution' of your dissertation or thesis and are prepared to 'stand or fall' by it.

Concluding section and references

Often, as Gatrell and Turnbull (2003) have observed, the weakest elements of student dissertations/theses, whether at undergraduate, masters or PhD level, are the conclusions and recommendations. This is unsurprising. By the time you reach the concluding section of your work you are likely to be tired, fed up and pressed for time. However, the conclusions section is really important. This is because, often, examiners turn first to the conclusions section (to gain an initial idea of what the thesis is about) before they read the whole document through from beginning to end. Thus, if the conclusions section has been hastily put together and does not reflect the quality of work demonstrated in the rest of the thesis, the examiner will get off to an unfortunate start, which does not create the good impression that your work may deserve. Your conclusions section should be more than just a rushed and final statement but should be a logical outcome of what you have said previously.

What should go in the concluding section?

Below are some suggestions about how you might structure your conclusions section, which will be helpful at whatever academic level you are working. These are as follows:

- Remind the reader of the purpose of your dissertation/thesis – recap your aims/research questions and make sure that they 'fit' with those espoused in your introductory section.
- Neatly *and succinctly* summarize the middle bits of your thesis – what you have done, how and why you did it and what you learned/discovered.
- In the context of your findings and the work of others, clearly specify the contribution(s) you have made in relation to your research question. Remember that the originality, or contribution, of your work does not have to be equivalent to Einstein's Theory of Relativity. But if you have thought about something in a new light, or done some empirical research which no one has done in quite the same way, you can claim this as a 'contribution', even if this relates very locally – perhaps to the marketing plan at your place of work.
- You may wish to say something about the limitations of your research. Alternatively, or additionally, you could also include this in a final section on 'building on your research' – the 'limitations' can be dealt with in the context of further research required.
- Finally, especially if you are doing a 'work-based' assignment, you might choose to make some recommendations for policy, or for workplace practices, which *must relate specifically* to what you have discussed earlier in the assignment.

What should *not* go in the concluding section

If you look up the word 'conclusion' in a thesaurus, you will find that this is defined variously as 'summing up', 'wrapping up', 'the finish', 'the end'. This ought to provide a clue as to what goes in this section, which should be short and sweet and should relate to what has gone before – no new topics or issues should be raised in the conclusion.

Reference section

I have already underlined (in the section on writing assignments) the importance of factoring in enough time at the end of your project to allow you to read through and edit carefully, thus ensuring that you hand in a tidy, polished piece of work with consistency in style, headings and numbering of figures/tables. It is especially important to check that your references are neatly and accurately presented. This is because academics often flick through the reference section before they begin to read the dissertation/thesis as this will give them a quick and overall impression of the academic areas with which you have engaged. Many academics set great store by neat and tidy references, so it is important to ensure that you are following the accepted style within your faculty (consult your course handbook or website to check this out); ensure that names are spelled correctly and that dates and page numbers are included. It will get you off to a good start with your reader/examiner if you try to ensure that your reference section is 'spot on'!

Keep to your timetable/deadlines

As Boyle (2005: 311) suggests,

> The final, and perhaps most important piece of advice that can be offered is that once you have done all of this work, make sure you hand it in on time!

Writing a dissertation or thesis: summary of key points

- Choose a topic which poses a legitimate research problem, is feasible, sensibly scoped and of interest to you.
- If you are doing a work-based dissertation, think through carefully what the consequences of your research might be before you begin – you do not want your thesis to limit your career!
- Begin writing from the start, and establish a study routine.
- Leave plenty of time for your concluding section and do not introduce new topics in this section.
- Ensure that your thesis is submitted on time.

4

Plagiarism, referencing and originality

What is plagiarism and why does it matter? • Plagiarism: summary of key points • Originality • Intellectual property • Why student work is vulnerable (at any academic level) • Originality and protecting your own intellectual property: summary of key points

As promised earlier, at the end of this chapter I intend to go into some detail about what is meant by the terms 'plagiarism' and 'originality'. To begin with, Chapter 4 will explain what is meant by plagiarism, why it is serious, and how you might avoid it. Plagiarism is a 'hot topic' in universities at the moment and understanding what it entails might be particularly important for part-time students who are not on campus. Part-timers may not be part of classroom discussions, or have access to the same peer networks to consult with other students about how to avoid plagiarism. I shall then go on to discuss the importance of protecting your own work, and consider what is meant by originality.

What is plagiarism and why does it matter?

The dictionary definition of plagiarism describes it as: 'the appropriation of ideas, passages etc., from another work or author'. In university terms, plagiarism means attempting to pass off the written work of another person as your own *without giving them the credit to which they are due*. In general terms, this includes any of the following: copying the work of another student, getting someone else to write your assignments for you, or 'lifting' sentences or para- graphs from books, articles or the internet and inserting these in your own work without saying where you got them from, and without citing the author's name. Plagiarism could also include the taking of someone else's idea or discovery and pretending that it is yours.

Why is plagiarism serious?

The purpose of a university degree or diploma is to demonstrate to the rest of the world that an individual student is qualified to a particular level in a given subject. A university's reputation rests upon the maintaining of agreed stand- ards. In order to ensure that marks are fair and evenly distributed, work is often double marked within an institution. Additionally, all degree programmes will be scrutinized by an external examiner who works at another institution, is an expert in the field, and is unlikely to be personally known to any of the stu- dents. Given the amount of trouble that is taken to try and ensure fair and appropriate levels of marking, it is understandable that universities do not wish to be seen to be giving qualifications to students who have not completed the required work, or who have copied work from others, because there would then be a risk that all qualifications awarded might lose credibility. An institution would never intentionally, therefore, accept work that has been plagiarized and would never knowingly award a degree to a student who has submitted work which is not their own. (For a useful further discussion and definition of plagiarism try Booth *et al.* 1995:169.)

For this reason, plagiarism has always been an issue in the university setting, and even in the past, students who copied chunks from books and inserted these into written work without referencing them, or who copied one anoth- er's work, were risking problems. Presently, however, plagiarism is more of a 'hot potato' than it has ever been. This is because academics are worried that the internet has made it relatively effortless for students to pass off the work of others as their own. Using the web, students can easily cut and paste the work of other writers into their own assignments without referencing. It is also much simpler than it was to purchase ready-made, complete assignments over the internet. In some cases these 'ready-made' assignments are sufficiently generic for students to apply them to standard courses. In other instances, it is possible to commission tailor-made assignments from writers who will apply their knowledge to a given question on the student's behalf.

Universities are therefore 'on the look out' for plagiarism and if they can find evidence of it, they will take action against the student concerned. Detection software now exists so that academics who are suspicious can run a piece of work through this to check for plagiarism. If a plagiarized paragraph or sen- tence exists in any form on the internet (and there are hundreds of journal and newspaper databases as well as individual websites) it will probably be picked up. If the work has been copied from a book, or from another student, this is also high-risk. Academics can be very precise people with long memories. If they read something four years ago they will probably remember it. So submitting an essay that was written by someone else who did your course, or something similar, several years ago, might still be risky. Sometimes this might mean the lowering of a mark, or the requirement to resubmit a piece of work. However, some universities have a 'one strike and out' policy, and if they can prove beyond reasonable doubt a case of plagiarism they might suspend or even remove the perpetrator from her/his degree programme. Most institutions will have a policy, which will probably be published on their website. Read it carefully, so that you know the rules – and as a rule of thumb, avoid plagiarism at all costs. Even if you are behind with your work and feeling desperate (in which case read Chapter 6 of this book), plagiarism is not an answer because it might put your whole degree at risk and is just not worth it.

Why students plagiarize

Part-time students who plagiarize the work of others usually do so for one, or more, of the reasons given below:

* They do not understand what is meant by plagiarism.
* They are unable to distinguish between their own ideas and those of other people.
* They have no idea how seriously plagiarism will be regarded by their university.
* They are behind with their work, and feeling desperate.
* They believe that certain types of plagiarism (lifting things off the net or copying the work of other students) do not 'count'.
* They believe that they will not be caught out.

How to draw upon the work of others without plagiarizing, or being accused of plagiarism

Inevitably, when you are writing assignments, dissertations or theses, you will be drawing upon the work of others. The higher the level of your degree, the more widely you will be expected to have read. For those doing undergraduate degrees, and for some postgraduate qualifications, a reading list (and maybe even the course texts) will be provided. However, you will be given credit for reading more widely. For masters, MPhil and PhD students, there is an expectation that you will do your own literature searches, exploring online databases and library collections for yourselves. Usually, the more you read and the better able you are to demonstrate an awareness of a variety of perspectives in your field, the higher your marks will be.

The basic rule when discussing the work of others is to be sure that you give them due credit for any ideas and/or quotations which are theirs. The purpose of identifying who 'owns' the concepts to which you refer in your assignment/ thesis is twofold: firstly; it means that written ideas, 'or intellectual property', are protected, and are associated with the person who wrote them. Additionally, anyone who is interested in following up a quote, or an idea that you have used in your assignment/thesis, can go and find it in the article or book from which it was originally taken. In your university work, therefore, you need to ensure that you have clearly and neatly referenced the work of others. The two most common styles of referencing are 'Harvard' and 'Vancouver'. Harvard references (the style used in this book and in the example below) reference directly in the text. Vancouver, which is probably less frequently used, references by use of footnotes. Your course handbook or website will tell you which style your university prefers, and should provide you with examples.

Reporting the views of others in your text

In brief there are two ways in which you might employ other writers' work in your text. You might simply wish to discuss an idea, or a set of ideas, that you have read elsewhere, but without quoting directly from the author. In such cases, you need only include in your text the name of the person to whom the idea belongs, and the year in which the book or article was written. So, for example, in a thesis about working mothers, you might suggest that:

> Hakim (2000) suggests that employed women who are also mothers are less committed to their paid work than are men, or women without children. Gatrell (2005) challenges this notion, arguing that a woman's job is often an important part of her social identity, regardless of whether or not she is a mother.

Your list of references would appear at the end of your thesis, in alphabetical order. If you are unsure where, or how, Hakim and Gatrell might fit into this list, have a look at the reference section at the back of this book.

Quoting the views of others in your text

If you wanted to discuss the issue under consideration in more detail, or to illustrate a particular point, you might then include a quote. In this case, you would carefully copy the relevant piece into your text, and add the author's last name, the year of publication, and the page number. In your thesis about working mothers, therefore, you might go on to say:

> Drawing upon her own research, Gatrell argues: 'Mothers demonstrated that they were deeply committed to their profession, going to great lengths to enable them to continue in employment. Women carried on with their paid work despite ill-health, public criticism, discriminatory

practices in the workplace and the guilt that they felt about leaving their children in the care of others.'

(Gatrell 2005: 216)

The attribution of quotes is important. As you are reading and taking notes for your thesis/assignment, be careful that you distinguish between where you have summarized what you have read in your own words, and where you have copied something directly from the text. In each case, be sure to attach the relevant details. If you know who said what, and where you read it, this can save you a good deal of time and pain later on. There is nothing worse than needing to use a quote in your assignment/thesis and being obliged to trawl though several articles (or worse, books) trying to find the page number.

If you reference properly, you can safely use the published ideas of others in your own work. You can build on their arguments, or critique these. You might, for example, be producing a dissertation on employers' attitudes to employed mothers. As long as you were clear, in your text, which arguments were your own and which derived from the ideas of others, you could not be accused of plagiarism. You would therefore be free to compare and contrast your own discoveries to the findings of (say) Gatrell (2005) and Hakim (2000), and hopefully would be commended for doing so.

The value of knowing that your work is all your own

So far, in relation to plagiarism, I have talked only of the university's requirement that your work should be all your own. There is, of course, an additional benefit, which is a personal one. The ability to distinguish between your own and others' ideas is important. It not only protects you from the possibility that you may (however unintentionally) be accused of trying to pass off others' work as your own. More positively, it also ensures that you are able to recognize your own achievements. You will be clear about where you have built upon the work of others, and where you have begun to develop your own thinking. You will derive a great deal of satisfaction from the knowledge that your degree has been earned as a result of what *you* have achieved, and is not due in part to the work of other students or writers. Being clear about what is your own work and what is derivative will also enable you to recognize it when *you* have come up with something original, which becomes increasingly important as you work your way up the higher education ladder, and is essential if you are aiming for a PhD.

Plagiarism: summary of key points

- Plagiarism means attempting to pass off the written work of others without giving them the credit to which they are due.
- It is considered by universities to be a serious issue, because academic institutions are concerned to protect the integrity of their degree programmes.
- Students usually plagiarize because they are behind with their work, do not realize how seriously plagiarism will be taken by their institution and do not believe that they will be found out.
- To avoid plagiarism, you must ensure that you fully reference all your sources.
- Avoiding plagiarism means you can derive great satisfaction from knowing your work is all your own.

Originality

For all those readers who are working towards a part-time PhD, and for some who are doing masters or MPhil/MLitt degrees, the notion of 'originality' will be very important. The word 'original' will feature in all handbooks or websites which deal with the requirements for the award of a doctorate. As noted in the introduction, the number of students registering to do doctorates on a part-time basis has risen sharply over the past decade and many readers of this book might be doing, or thinking about doing, a PhD. For this reason – and before I go on to discuss the importance of protecting your own, original ideas, I will consider what is meant by the concept of 'original'.

As Philips and Pugh (2005) point out, examiners are not expecting all PhD students to be Einstein. They further observe that even Einstein did not change the world through what he had written in his PhD thesis, which made a 'sensible' contribution to Brownian Motion Theory. His theory on relativity came later. Thus, Einstein's thesis was an interesting and original piece of work which was enough to gain him the title 'Dr', and which put him in a good position to develop his ideas in the future.

So what do examiners mean by 'original'? Inevitably your work will draw upon the work of other scholars, and your ideas will develop from theories and concepts which already exist. In order to gain your PhD, however, you must demonstrate that you have made an 'original contribution', which will have a place in the scholarly literature in your field.

For those undertaking empirical research, part of the 'originality' of what you are doing will be in your results, and in the analysis of your data. Since this is your own research, no one will have written about it before you do (though do see the section below on protecting your intellectual property). However, you will still need to be clear how, and where, your research fits in to what has been done before, and to investigate how far it accords with, or departs from, what has already been written. If your work is entirely theoretical, you will need to be able to articulate precisely how and where your arguments build on what has already been written, and in what way your research presents things in a new light. 'Originality' need not necessarily mean that your research will change the world, and your contribution might be a relatively modest suggestion about how things might be viewed differently. However, you must be able to demonstrate how your research moves forward the debate in your field, and (as observed above) be clear about which ideas belong to other people, and which are your own.

There are a number of publications which provide further and helpful consideration of how you might define 'originality' and 'contribution'. I suggest the most helpful and straightforward of these are Booth *et al.* (1995), Murray (2002) and Philips and Pugh (2005).

Intellectual property

Having discussed the concept of originality, I will now move on to consider the issue of intellectual property. The focus of this section is on the value of your own work, and of your own precious ideas. Your work is worth something and you need to know how, why, and from whom, to protect it. The term 'intellectual property' is often used in connection with the work of established academics. Once a piece of scholarly work has been published, especially if this is in the form of a book, or a paper in an academic journal, the writer's name is attached to it. Anyone who wishes to discuss the ideas it contains must fully cite and reference the work (or be accused of plagiarism!), because it is the author's 'intellectual property'.

Most established academics know the value of their ideas. They may be very careful about how and where they share these while they are still unpublished. Additionally, academics who have been working in a particular 'field' begin to build up a reputation for their expert knowledge. It therefore becomes increasingly difficult for 'newcomers' to encroach on what established academics are doing without (at the very least) referencing the originator of a particular piece of work. It would, for example, be ill-advised for a scholar wishing to publish on the topic of occupational stress not to refer to the work of Cary Cooper, the well-known psychologist. This is because Professor Cooper is a leading authority on stress and employment. Were anyone to omit his name from a publication about workplace stress, reviewers and/or publishers would probably pick this up long before the book or article went to press, and suggest that Cooper's work should be referenced.

Protecting your own 'intellectual property'

What about your own work? It is easy for students to assume that their own academic work is of little value to anyone other than themselves. For full-time students, there are many opportunities to discuss their work in class as they progress their studies. Advice given to part-time students often focuses on the need to find and build up networks with others at the same stage, working in similar areas. This is because their limited (or non-existent) presence on campus can lead part-timers to feel isolated and demotivated, sometimes leading, eventually, to withdrawal from their programme. Advice about establishing networks is therefore relevant and valuable (and you will find it in this book in Chapter 2). However, it comes with a health warning.

Undergraduate and masters/postgraduate students

The more work you invest in your part-time degree, the more valuable it is – both to you and to others. If, at this stage, you are working at undergraduate level, or just beginning postgraduate study, you might not imagine a circumstance where you would seek to publish your work as a book or a journal article. But for those of you doing dissertations, the possibility of coming up with something 'new' is there, and you might find yourself, at the end of your degree programme, wanting to try and publish your research before moving on to a masters degree or even a PhD. Even if you are not thinking of trying to publish your work at the moment, the prospect of someone else publishing your research, and putting their name to it, might make you stop and think about how you might try to protect it.

PhD students

For those readers who are working towards a PhD, the concept of 'intellectual property' is a serious one. I have already discussed the importance of producing work which may be defined as 'original' in order to gain your doctorate. However, your work does not become 'original' overnight, at the point when you are due to submit your thesis. From the outset, as you develop your literature review and begin to write, you are also developing your own ideas and your own thinking. It takes six to seven years for most part-time PhD students to gain their qualifications and many undervalue the work that they are doing prior to their viva. It is important to recognize from the start that your growing thesis is your intellectual property. If someone takes your ideas and publishes them elsewhere, this might substantially reduce the value of your research – or, even worse, render it worthless.

Why student work is vulnerable (at any academic level)

We have already discussed the reasons why students plagiarize the work of others. For those same reasons it would also be perfectly possible for someone to plagiarize your work – regardless of what stage you are at in your study (though the higher the level of your degree, the more serious the consequences for you). In addition to the causes given above, students' work may sometimes be plagiarized on the following basis:

- The work has not been published anywhere and the student is not established in the field so it would be difficult for the student to prove that the ideas were hers/his in the first place.
- Students are not always aware of the value of their work and do not always take the appropriate steps to protect it.
- Students voluntarily give away their ideas.

I will deal with these causes of plagiarism of student work in order.

It is difficult for the student to prove that the ideas were hers/his in the first place

One of the first steps here is to be certain that you are clear yourself, in the context of your written work, about what are your own ideas. (I have already discussed how to distinguish between your own ideas, or research, and that of others, in the section above.) Make sure that you name and date all your work. With modern technology it is possible to attach a 'header' section above each page with your name and the date right through your assignment, dissertation or thesis. (It is accepted that for some degree programmes, submission must be anonymous. However, it is highly unlikely that you would need to worry about your ideas being 'stolen' in the process of examination, which is very carefully monitored and which does not usually involve the retention of scripts, assignments or theses, by staff.)

If you are sharing work with others as part of a discussion group (either face-to-face or online), or if you leave your work out on your desk and others see it, there will be no question about who it belongs to and when it was written if you name and date every page. At conferences, if the formal presentation of your work is accompanied by handouts, ensure that your name is on each of these, that you make a note of what you presented where, and what the date was on each occasion.

Student experience

I had written this research report, based on some research I had done in my workplace. It did not have my name on it and I had handed it around to one or two people to look at. Some weeks later, I was asked to attend a seminar given by this woman whom I knew vaguely, because colleagues thought I would be interested in what she had to say. They thought she was working in a similar field to my own. Imagine my feelings when I listened to her presenting as her own thoughts what were basically *my* ideas, from *my* report!

From that date on, I have been very careful about handing my unpublished work around, and I *always* put my name on everything.

(Alison, part-time postgraduate, Education)

Be aware of the value of your work and take appropriate steps to protect it

It is not the intention here to put you off discussing your work with other students, or to discourage you from presenting it at conferences or to colleagues. As noted in Chapter 2, part-time students need to take every opportunity to discuss their work with others and gain feedback from peers, since this is usually an integral element of full-time study and part-timers often miss out on it. However, the use of a little caution can go a long way. Discussing your work with fellow students who are part of your study group, or your online discussion group, is useful and appropriate. (Even so, there is no need to give them copies of your entire assignment/thesis – just let them look at the section which is relevant to your discussion.) However, sharing your ideas in detail with people whom you do not know – for example in cyberspace – could be risky.

Student experience

I was at the start of writing my thesis on religion and employment and I was engaged in lively, interesting online chats with people from all over the world in a variety of sites on religion and life in general. One of the teachers in my faculty said that the topic of my thesis was exciting and original, which was great. She was horrified though when I told her that I had sent electronic copies of my work, and of all my references, to anyone who was interested because she thought my ideas would be relatively easy for someone else to pick up on. And since I was doing my thesis part-time, another student could have gone with the ideas before I even got halfway through. Since then I have been more circumspect about sharing my work and I no longer circulate multiple electronic copies among groups of people in online chat rooms. Now I put my name on everything I write and I usually chat online with individual students rather than to a general audience.

(Alex, part-time MPhil in Organizational Behaviour)

Don't give away your ideas voluntarily – plagiarism by other students

Students sometimes find that someone else has taken advantage of their good nature. At the request of others, they loan out their work, which the borrower then submits, presents, or publishes in his/her own name, without giving due credit to the student author. So one reason why students' work is plagiarized by others is because the student herself, or himself, has given the perpetrator permission to use it.

If someone asks for a copy of your written work, or seeks to use it for any purpose (in teaching, or to gain some ideas), think very carefully before you say 'yes'. Ask the borrower what s/he intends to use it for, whether s/he plans to give due credit to you, and when it will be returned to you. It is not uncommon for students to 'borrow' assignments or dissertations when they are behind, or stuck with their own work. This is a risky business, because if the plagiarizer is caught out, the lender can also find herself or himself in trouble (see Jane's example below). This might seem a bit unfair but, as noted earlier in this chapter, universities are keen to protect the integrity of the degrees they award, and if that means taking firm measures to prevent the occurrence of plagiarism in the future, they will do so. If one of your peers seeks to borrow your work, the best way forward is to offer to talk about what is required, but not to agree to lend your assignments/dissertation. Where possible, avoid lending electronic copies of anything you write. If you really feel it is necessary to lend your work out, offer only a hard copy (you can always put it in the post), lend only the section which is under discussion, be clear that you would like your paper to be returned and agree a date.

Student experience

I was doing a module on the public sector which was part of a six-year degree. I was having a great time on the course and got on fantastically well with my course colleagues, whom I met in class on a Saturday morning once a month. After the session we always went to the pub then sometimes we would go for a walk. Some of them were very bright – one was a doctor who had small children and was always really friendly and chatty, though I knew she was really pressured at work. Where I always did the reading though, and got my work in on time, others struggled or could not be bothered. And my doctor friend got in a real mess with her work, so she asked if she could borrow my stuff. I didn't even think about it – I just handed over my essays and let her get on with it.

The consequences of this though were just awful. The course tutor kept us on after class on the Saturday and really let us have it. She said it was obvious what we had been doing and pointed out the rules on plagiarism which were right there on the website. She said that we were both risking our place on the course and she told me that I should have more pride in my own work. The doctor didn't really care. She said that she was just doing the course to 'learn the jargon and beat the managers at their own game'. But I was just mortified. The module could be taken on its own or as part of a six-year-long undergraduate degree, which I was halfway through. The thought of losing my place – and all that time and money I'd spent – made me feel ill. And to make things worse, my friend was really 'off' with me for the rest of the course and we lost touch afterwards. I think she thought I had told on her or something (though I had not), so I kind of lost a friend as well. I must admit that I've always been hard-working and all through school and college I happily let other people copy my work. But I never realized how serious it was, and I would never do it again.

(Jane, part-time postgraduate, Public Sector Finance)

Plagiarism on the part of academic staff

Students do not normally need to worry about their work being plagiarized by university staff, who in 99 per cent of cases have sufficient ideas of their own, and enough integrity, not to wish to plagiarize student work to help their own careers. (It is not, however, uncommon for a tutor/supervisor to suggest that s/he writes something jointly with a student. This is often a great opportunity to work and publish with an experienced, professional academic.)

Very occasionally, however, as in the example below, faculty might seek permission to use a student's work, and if this happens to you it is perfectly reasonable for you to seek further information about why they want to do this. If you are at all unhappy, you might explain politely that you are intending to publish or teach the work yourself, but that it is still in development, so you would prefer not to loan them a copy at this time.

Student experience

I am a nurse, and I did a dissertation as part of my part-time masters in Sociology of Health, and in our department they viva a sample of students and I was one of those who got picked out. The topic of my work was on teenage pregnancy in the UK. The viva went well and the examiner was really nice to me. At the end of the viva, she asked if she could keep a copy of my dissertation to use in teaching. At the time, I was really flattered so I said yes and gave it to her. It was only afterwards that I thought: What have I done? I have just given this woman the dissertation which it has taken me a year to write, and I thought I might try and get it published in a nursing journal.

And I am not exactly flush with money, so if nothing else I could have had the sense to ask her if *I* could teach a session on teenage pregnancy, and be paid something for it. I talked to a friend and she suggested I write a letter, explaining that I was pleased the examiner liked the work, but that I hoped to publish it myself and would prefer if she did not use it in any written work of hers. I got a fairly curt reply back, with the thesis, saying that she had had no intention to do this. The thing is, the story doesn't end there. About two years later, I was in the bookshop and I noticed a book on health issues and teenage girls. The author was my examiner. I looked through it carefully, and it was obvious that my dissertation had not been used. But I do wonder . . . what might have happened if I hadn't written that letter?

(Jane, part-time masters in Sociology of Health)

Originality and protecting your own intellectual property: summary of key points

- Students working at all levels may produce original work by examining something from a new angle or doing some empirical research. PhD students, however, must make an original contribution to scholarly knowledge and should be able to articulate precisely how their arguments build upon what is already written and where they depart from existing literature and/ or present things in a new light.
- Your research is your own intellectual property and you should take steps to protect it. You can do this in several ways: name and date all your work (attach a header section to each page throughout your written work with your name and the date on it), be cautious about sharing your ideas in cyberspace with groups who do not identify themselves and whom you do not know, and avoid lending your work to other students for the purposes of copying – even if they are behind with their work and desperate.

5

Coping with exams

Worrying about exams • Preparing for exams • Improving your performance on the day of the exam • Coping with exams: summary of key points

This chapter is a short one, but it is important, because it is devoted to the prospect of being assessed through examination. In this section I will discuss why examinations might be stressful and offer some practical guidance on how you can reduce your anxiety levels. In particular, I will make a series of suggestions which can help you enhance your exam performance, and raise your exam grades.

Worrying about exams

One of the most worrying aspects of any academic study (regardless of whether this is part-time or full-time) is the undertaking of examinations. A recent study of examinations and stress, which took the blood pressure readings of students before and after they sat examinations (Hughes 2005), demonstrated that all students experienced higher blood pressure readings before end-of-term examinations than afterwards, suggesting that exams are stressful for everyone. Interestingly, the students of high academic ability (who might, arguably, have been expected to be less worried about exams than their peers) demonstrated the highest levels of pre-examination stress, perhaps because the expectations about the level of their achievement would be greater than for those in the middle levels of the group.

Most people worry about exams. Increasingly, programmes are designed to include a higher level of coursework with less emphasis on formal examination. While this is beneficial in that it allows students to develop their thinking and demonstrate consistency in their work without exam pressure, it inevitably means that exams are less frequent, and become more worrying as a result. However, many programmes still retain an examination element, with course work throughout the year and exams at the end. Students undertaking business degrees, Open University degrees and many clinical qualifications will be required to take exams. Although some exams allow the use of a PC and some allow you to take reference books into the exam room, most involve the old-fashioned method of sitting at a desk for three hours in silence, answering unseen questions and writing an exam script by hand, which then disappears into the ether, never to be seen again. For some students (usually those who have only recently left university or school, and who are doing part-time study alongside first jobs), memories of being examined might be quite recent. For others, however (usually mature students who have started, or returned to, higher education after a break of many years), exams are a dim and unpleasant memory. For this group, the thought of entering an exam room again after all that time can seem terrifying. As Scott Holtham observes, 'Exam nerves haunted me in a way I had never experienced in the cavalier days of my youth' (Holtham 2000: 75).

Before I go on to talk about how to approach (and improve) the exam experience, it is worth considering the question: what are exams for, and whom do they benefit? It is easy to imagine why a university might want to examine students in a formal setting. An examination is a useful way of testing a student's understanding of her/his subject, and it may also act as 'quality' check. If a whole class has struggled with a particular question, or concept, then that sends a message to the institution that it may need to look at the way the subject is taught. Written exams are also an easy way of checking that students' coursework is all their own. There is a general assumption that, for many students, their average grade will drop around 7 to 10 per cent in an exam situation. So if a student is used to gaining a grade of around 60 per cent in assignments, her/his exam marks are likely to be around 50 to 53 per cent. Thus, if a student has been gaining an average of 68 per cent in coursework, but achieves only 36 per cent in an exam, the question is raised as to how much of the coursework was the student's own.

While it is easy to understand why universities like exams, it is more difficult, on the face of it, to see the benefits to students. I am going to argue, however, that there are some positive aspects to taking exams. In the first place, an exam is over in a short time. Although you may have to revise for it, it may not take you as long, or be as painstaking, as writing another assignment, or even undertaking a dissertation, which might be the alternative. Additionally, it does give you the chance to prove that you are comfortable with your own subject – an exam is your chance to show the examiner what you know. This is an important point, because students often know more than they give themselves credit for. Poor exam marks (as I shall discuss in the next section) are often bestowed as a result of poor exam performance, not because the student lacks the required knowledge.

Why are exams so stressful?

Exams are stressful because candidates feel that they have little or no control over the process. They will be tested, but they have no advance knowledge of exactly what they will be tested on. This feels worrying because they are unsure of what to revise, and fear that they might forget something really important on the big day. Candidates may be tested in unfamiliar, and perhaps uncomfortable, settings where they have no control over lighting, temperature, seating and so on. Especially for part-time students, there may be a requirement to travel to an examination centre in a city that they do not know, and to take the exam alongside other people whom they do not know.

Most exams last for three hours, a length of time which may appear dauntingly long before the exam begins but far too short at the end, especially if not all questions have been answered fully. Finally, the sense that candidates have no control over the exam process is intensified by the fact that exam marking is shrouded in mystery. Once an 'official' exam paper has been handed in, candidates are unlikely ever to see it again. A percentage or grade will be awarded, but this is rarely accompanied by any feedback, so it is difficult to analyse how and where examinees did well, or badly.

Additionally, and perhaps most pertinently, exams are stressful because we do them so rarely. Imagine that you had passed your driving test, but subsequently got in your car and drove in busy traffic on one occasion only, each year (and this maybe after a twenty-year break). In such circumstances, your annual journey as a driver could be quite stressful. You might, additionally, be worried about your effectiveness on the road. If you wanted to improve your driving performance, the logical solution to your concerns would be to practise driving more often. This is exactly the situation with exams, and the best way to reduce your anxiety levels and to enhance your performance is to practise answering questions in (as close as you can get to) exam conditions, as often as possible before the event. As Joanna argues, you can improve your exam performance with practice.

Student experience

No matter what else I have got on, I do make a point of attending exam revision days. The Open University is really good at providing help and advice about exam revision techniques and this is definitely something that can be learned. I've got much better at taking exams over the last six years. I strongly believe that you don't need luck. With exams, what you need are the three 'Ps' – Prior Planning and Preparation avoids pathetic poor performance!

(Joanna, part-time undergraduate, Psychology)

Preparing for exams

Most importantly, you need to practise answering exam questions to time. Seek out some old exam questions. If you can't get hold of old exam papers, don't worry. Either ask your course convenor if s/he can set you and others a practice paper, or use one of the 'question and answer' sections included at the end of chapters in one of your course texts. The purpose here is not simply to check out what you know about the subject (though this is one way of doing that!) but principally to get you used to organizing your thoughts on paper within a short timescale. Shut yourself away for an hour or 45 minutes, or whatever time is allowed for your subject, and answer the question as effectively as you can. Set an alarm or timer so that your timing is accurate and don't be tempted to stop until your hour/45 minutes is up. Conversely, don't be tempted to continue – in the 'real' exam, your timing needs to be exact for each question, otherwise you will be unable to finish your paper – and the examiner cannot give you marks for points you have not had time to make. In the 'real' exam, you may need to be strict with yourself and move on to the next question, even if the answer you are working on is unfinished. You will receive some credit for giving a partial answer, but nothing at all for questions which you have not started.

Begin your 'exam' by *reading your question carefully* and doing a short plan of what you need to include in your answer. Only plan to put in the main points – you cannot fit everything you know into one exam question so you will need to make choices, otherwise you will run out of time and may omit something important. Remember, the examiner is not only testing your memory. S/he wants to know that you are able to collect your thoughts together, and answer the question that s/he has set. Do not answer the question you revised for – answer the question that is on the paper. Where possible, show that you can associate the right author with the concepts/theories you discuss. If using numbers or tables, ensure that you refer to these within the text, so that the examiner understands what they are there for.

What is the examiner looking for?

As well as trying to obtain a sense of what you know, the examiner is interested in testing *how effectively you can analyse problems*, and how well you can communicate your thoughts, when working to a tight timescale. It is not how *much* you know on the day that counts, but how well you can *apply* it.

For those aiming for a good mark at undergraduate level, and for most masters students, it may be that there is no single 'right' answer to the question set. The examiner might hope that you will consider the topic from a number of angles, before drawing some sensible conclusions. To gain good marks, you will be expected to have considered your argument in the light of your learning on the course. You will need to draw on and summarize the views of particular scholars to substantiate what you are saying. In the first paragraph of your answer, state briefly how you plan to structure your essay and how this relates to the question. This will not only guide the examiner, but will serve to keep you on track. As you write, use subheadings to help you structure what you are trying to say. These will also help guide the examiner through your answer. Try and allow time, in the final paragraph, to summarize your answer and restate how you have answered all parts of the question. Remember to read through your exam paper carefully, and answer only those questions which you are required to. In the stress of the exam situation, students often answer more questions, or sections of questions, than they need to. This does not gain them any extra marks, but may waste precious time.

Aim to finish each question with two or three minutes to spare. This will allow you to read through it at the end and check for mistakes. Make sure you get into the habit of neatly writing your name on your answer sheet, and ensuring that you have clearly marked on your sheet which question you are answering. Unless you are allowed to use a keyboard in your exam, write by hand and in pen to do your practice paper. This will help you get used to the unfamiliar feel of hand writing before the exam takes place, as in Scott's case, below:

> When the time came [to sit my exam], my problem lay not in knowing how to express myself concisely but in the physical process of writing the answer down. I rarely use a pen for much more than writing the odd cheque or marking the students' work at school, neither of which requires the physical dexterity that essay writing demands. Halfway through the three-hour exam, with one essay done and another to be begun, my right hand had suddenly developed arthritic symptoms and reduced my writing speed to a snail's pace. The ideas were queuing up to be put down, but I was at the mercy of my aching fingers. If exam practice is useful in any sense it is for this – get used to writing for a long time with a pen.
>
> (Holtham 2000: 76)

If you can get your course convenor or tutor/supervisor to look at your practice script, so much the better, but if not you could ask course colleagues to do this for you (and you could reciprocate). If this is not an option because you are studying in relative isolation, don't worry. Once you have finished your 'practice exam', you can refer to your revision texts and notes, using the following checklist:

Exam checklist
- Do you think you understood what the examiner was asking for? Have you covered all the key points?
- Did you complete the question on time?
- Is your answer clear and legible (did you underline headings and spell names correctly)?

- Did you remember to reference the main topics, citing academic authors and frameworks where appropriate?
- What could you do differently to improve your performance another time?

(Adapted from Gatrell and Turnbull 2003)

Then repeat the exercise with a new question. Resist the temptation simply to read and discuss the question – make yourself sit down and answer it in writing and to time on each occasion. Do this as many times as you need to until you feel that answering questions under exam conditions is starting to feel more comfortable and familiar, and that you are able to complete your answer in the given timeframe and get all the main points in. Get into the habit of writing as neatly as possible and ensure that you have written a heading and/or the number of your question, at the start of each question. This may sound obvious, but students often forget when under pressure in the 'real' exam.

Example of how to construct an exam answer

I am going to provide an example which is related to a specific topic, but the principles of which you can apply and adapt to your own topic. Imagine you were doing an undergraduate degree in Community Education Practice, and you were sitting an exam on this subject. You have an hour in which to write up your answer. Your exam question might be:

Are values and principles important for Community Education Practitioners?

In your answer, your examiner would expect you to demonstrate the following basic and relevant knowledge:

- that you understand what is meant, in the field of Community Education, by values and principles;
- that you are aware of the specific set of professional values and principles to which Community Education practitioners must adhere (namely Community Education Validation and Endorsement).

In addition, in order for you to gain good marks, the examiner would hope that you might:

- debate what influence personal values and principles might (or might not) have on practice;
- show that you recognize, and have *analysed*, the potential for conflict between personal and professional values and principles;
- provide one short and relevant example, perhaps about health education in

the community (do not get sidetracked into talking about health – remember you are mentioning this only to illustrate, in brief, your points about values and principles);
* make recommendations about how practitioners might deal with the consequences of such a conflict.

In this answer, you would be given credit for substantiating your argument by drawing upon the work of Richardson and Wolfe (2001), *Principles and Practice of Informal Learning*, as this is the text which deals with the issue of values and principles in Community Education. This would make for a well-structured answer, would more than satisfy the examiner, and would be achievable in the time given. It responds directly to the question that has been set and does not include any superfluous information. (You might be very knowledgeable about health education in the community, but this is not relevant here *except* in the context of values, principles and your short example.)

Improving your performance on the day of the exam

Suppose you have completed your practice papers and you have now reached the day of the exam. There are a number of important things to remember on the day. The following tips for exam success are adapted from Gatrell and Turnbull (2003), which offers a more detailed chapter on exam success. This book was written with business students in mind, but the general advice on taking exams is relevant whatever your discipline.

On the day of the exam   Gatrell and Turnbull's ten golden rules for success
1 *Make sure you are certain about the location of the exam* and allow plenty of travel time to avoid stress on the day.
2 *Synchronize your watch with the exam room clock.*
3 Once you may begin, *read the exam paper through carefully from start to finish*. Check that there aren't any questions on the reverse. Ensure that you are clear exactly which questions you are supposed to answer.
4 *Once you have read* all *the questions on the paper, decide which ones you are going to attempt.* Go for the 'best' first, and so on in order of preference. It will improve your confidence if you get off to a good start.
5 *Think hard about what the examiner is asking for* and draw up a plan before starting each question. This will help you to decide what to include in your answer, and (just as importantly) what to leave out. Include only *relevant* information, not everything you know.

6   *Apportion your time properly.* You need enough time to construct your plan, write your answer, draw conclusions and read through what you have written.

7   *Make sure that your paper is presented as neatly as possible.* A clearly set out exam script gives the impression of a well organized student.

8   *Avoid looking at other candidates in the exam room.* If you are stuck, it is disconcerting to see everyone else scribbling away. It can be equally disturbing to be aware of candidates in distress. This is *not* your responsibility. The invigilator will take action if necessary.

9   *Allow 5 to 10 minutes at the end of the exam for reading through.*

10 *Once the exam is over, forget it.* Let others do a 'post mortem' if they wish to but make your focus the next exam or, if your exams have finished, celebrate!

Coping with exams: summary of key points

- Exams are stressful because candidates feel they have little control over the exam process, and because we take exams so rarely. By practising and developing your exam technique you can take control and improve your exam performance.
- Practise answering exam questions to time.
- Read the questions carefully – remember the examiner is not looking merely at how much you know, but how well you can apply it.
- If possible get your tutor/supervisor to give you feedback on your practice scripts.
- Follow Gatrell and Turnbull's ten golden rules on the day of the exam.

6

The mid-term blues: getting stuck, and staying on course

Falling behind with your work • Reasons why students get behind: summary of key points • Missed deadlines and coping with a muddle • Giving up • Reasons for non-completion of part-time study: summary of key points • Deciding not to complete: summary of key points • Picking up the threads and getting back on course • Why do we find writing so difficult? • Picking up the threads and starting to write again: summary of key points • What to do when things go wrong • When things go wrong: summary of key points

Many part-time postgraduate students experience a sense of frustration mid-way through their programme. It is acknowledged that, although everyone starts out with the best of intentions, many part-time students get disheartened at some point in their course. This may be because they fall behind with their work and find it difficult to pick things up again, or it may be because they have had to suspend their studies due to changes in their private or business lives. Equally, there may be students who have succeeded in keeping up with their work so far, but who find that the daily grind of managing part-time study alongside other aspects of their lives is wearing them down. Part-way through a programme of study, once the initial excitement has worn off, it is easy to feel fed up and demotivated – especially when it comes to writing assignments and dissertations.

Many study guides emphasize the need to keep on track and to stick to timetables, but offer limited advice about what to do when things have gone wrong, and you are already behind with your work. Some fail to acknowledge altogether that non-completion is a possibility. (Murray 2002 is an exception to this – her advice on writing is helpful to all but is probably especially helpful to those who are experiencing difficulties, or who have stopped writing altogether). In the following section, therefore, I intend to acknowledge how difficult it is to keep going over a long period when you are a part-time student, as well as how easy it is to get behind with academic work. I make some suggestions about how you might assess the level of slippage and how to manage your studies when a backlog of work has built up. Recognizing that non-completion may be the only option for some students, I address this issue and suggest what criteria you might use for making the decision about whether or not to continue part-time study.

For those who have decided to carry on, I then consider some techniques for getting back into the swing of things, and for picking up your studies after a break. This includes some specific advice about the practicalities and what options you might have for negotiating with your institution. I then make some specific suggestions about how you might refuel your enthusiasm and, in particular, how to make the process of writing of academic assignments, theses and dissertations less burdensome. This section will be useful for anyone who has to produce written work as part of their coursework, and the advice offered here is given in the context of the suggestions made in Chapter 3 on writing assignments, dissertations and theses. However, the main focus in Chapter 6 is on picking up your studies after a break and starting to write again, especially if you are suffering from 'writer's block'. Suggestions are made about what to do when you just can't seem to put pen to paper. This section draws on experiences from other students and also refers readers to 'companion' texts which will offer more detailed advice.

Chapter 6 then offers a section on 'what to do when things go wrong'. A section is included on 'deciding this is not for you' – how to deal with the situation where, midway though your programme, it becomes clear to you that successful completion is unlikely.

A discussion takes place about intimate relationships between students and faculty, and about sexual harassment. The chapter concludes with a discussion about when to take issue with your university, and how this may be done tactfully.

Falling behind with your work

If we lived in a perfect world, I would not need to write this chapter. Once you had begun your studies, everything would run along smoothly. Everyone would enjoy writing their assignments, finish their course on time and pass with good grades. Unfortunately, however, the reality of part-time study is rather different. As I have discussed in previous chapters, combining academic study with paid work, relationships, parenting and other commitments (such as a social life!) can be really hard. This is not helped by the fact that many part-time programmes can take years to complete, meaning that momentum has to be kept up over a long period of time. The submission of assignments and the passing of exams puts a huge pressure on those who are combining study with other things. And arguably, the pressure to 'keep going' becomes even more intense for those trying to write a dissertation, or a thesis, on a part-time basis. Many students enjoy reading around their topic and collecting their data, but feel completely overwhelmed as their deadline looms and they are expected to condense months of hard work into a 10,000- or 20,000-word dissertation. This is especially true for those who are producing lengthy pieces of research at MPhil or PhD level because the deadlines associated with assignments do not apply, and the skills involved in managing a piece of work which may be between 50,000 and 100,000 words cannot be underestimated. As Sachs (2002: 99, my emphasis) suggests, 'Writing a thesis can be characterised as the *ultimate* self-regulated learning task.'

Why part-time students fall behind

The longer you leave, it, the worse it gets. Picking up your studies after a break is probably the hardest part of part-time study. Once you have missed one deadline (even if you have gained permission for an extension), or if you have taken an 'official' break from study, catching up and getting started again can be very problematic. And the difficulty in picking up after getting behind or taking a break is probably the most common reason why part-timers fail to complete their courses.

Drop-out rates for part-time students usually 'peak' at two key stages in their studies. Attrition rates are often at their highest during the early stages of a course because a proportion of students who thought they had the time, money, or interest/motivation to undertake a programme of study soon realize that the course they have chosen is not for them. For this reason there will be a 'drop-out' rate during the early stages of most programmes, often before the first assignment is submitted. The remaining students will probably settle down and make good progress, handing in work and gradually getting to know student colleagues either face-to-face or online. By the middle of the registration period, however, some students will be falling behind. Inevitably, this group will find that getting back on track is really hard. For students who fail to hand in assignments on time, the deadlines for the next piece of work will begin to loom. Before they know it, the amount of work 'owed' by them to their institution will have built up to unmanageable proportions and the possibility of successful completion recedes into the distance.

For full-time residential students, keeping up with their work is usually (though not always) easier than it is for part-timers. This is not only because academic study is their main activity (most are full-time students doing part-time paid work, as opposed to part-time students who may be in full-time employment) but also because their institution will impose a routine upon them, ensuring that most write regularly and keep on top of course timetables. Peer pressure and support will also be on hand – a room-mate or study partner who might spur you on by asking how your assignment is progressing, or by suggesting an evening's study or a visit to the library. Things are much harder for part-time students who have to establish their own routine, who may not have fellow students 'on hand' to offer support, and who may need to put course work to one side for a period due to the pressure of other commitments.

It has to be admitted here that, for some part-time students, it seems to make no difference how complicated life becomes. Some will experience the most stressful and complicated life events, including job losses, divorce and serious health problems (either their own or those of other family members). Yet for this group, so long as they can hold a pen or press a letter on keyboard, they will continue to produce coursework no matter what happens. This is because they are usually enjoying their course and find the work stimulating and exciting. However, they may also have advantages that do not apply to you – dedicated study time offered by employers, greater financial flexibility, supportive partners/family. Some students may even relish the chance to be away from their everyday problems (either mentally while studying, or physically while away on a course), regarding part-time study as something of a solace. This group are usually determined to finish at all costs and will probably succeed.

For the majority of part-time students, however, life is less straightforward. During their programme of study, many will experience life events which demand attention and take the focus away from academic work, meaning that keeping up-to-date with written work becomes challenging. Falling behind for some students may begin when they struggle to meet the deadline for a single assignment, because they need to take a break while securing further funding, or due to crises at work or at home. However, the requesting of even a short extension on one piece of work often puts part-time students under impossible pressure. Once out of 'synch' with their academic timetable, the challenge of catching up becomes increasingly daunting because, as well as the assignment which is overdue, students are expected to be starting on the next piece of work. The initial slippage in the course timetable then starts to build up into an overwhelming backlog of work owed, and this quickly becomes impossible to catch up with. The pressure caused by the backlog of work owed is likely to exacerbate any study problems that they may be experiencing. Unfortunately, therefore, what begins with a request for an extension over just a few weeks can soon, and easily, build up to being a whole year behind. Imogen, who is undertaking a masters degree in Political Science, describes her own situation below:

Student experience

In the first year, I needed an extension for six weeks. And somehow, this led to my falling a whole *year* behind. I was determined to keep going though, and my tutor advised me to rejoin the course at the point my fellow students had reached. So in other words, I was working on 'current' assignments at the same time as all the others, with a view to catching up on the missing work when everyone else had finished. As it turned out, I was not the only student who had got behind and three of my colleagues and I formed a study group, each hosting a study visit in our own environment. For me, the responsibility of hosting the study visit was really important in keeping me motivated. The fact that we had a really supportive tutor/supervisor was also immensely helpful in focusing and inspiring me.

(Imogen, part-time masters in Political Science)

Many part-time students enjoy reading and fieldwork, but find it difficult to settle down and begin writing assignments or dissertations. The knowledge that you are getting further and further behind with written work can only serve to make these problems worse and may cause real 'writer's block'. In addition, the difficult circumstances which caused the delay in the first place might still be difficult. A new role at work, or a health problem, might consume your time and energy for a considerable period, meaning that your part-time study plans are placed on the 'back burner' for longer than you had originally planned. It is all too easy to find yourself getting further and further behind as the work mounts up.

For some students, the decision to take a break in study may be strategic, and extended. A particular event such as the obtaining of a demanding job or contract, the arrival of a baby, health or financial problems might mean the official suspension of studies for a period of time, with academic work put to one side while other things take precedence. For this group the decision to take a break is often a straightforward (though not ideal) choice: they either suspend their studies for a period of time, or withdraw from their programme altogether. Placing academic study on the 'back burner' at least has the advantage of leaving the options open.

Whatever the circumstances, however, being behind with academic work is both stressful and overwhelming. If assignments are supposed to be written in conjunction with taught elements of your programme, the memory of what was taught weeks or months ago quickly fades. Consequently, the assignment becomes increasingly difficult to produce, because you have forgotten some of the basic coursework and the core ideas that were part of it. Thus, you need to spend valuable time trying to familiarize yourself with past course topics before you feel you can start.

Writing your thesis part-time

Arguably, the pressure to 'keep going' becomes even more intense for those trying to write a thesis on a part-time basis, especially if you have decided to take a break part way through. This is especially true for those who are working on postgraduate research degrees, trying to produce a scholarly piece of work over a longer period, when the only 'interim' deadlines are those which are self-imposed. As a part-time student, even if you are keeping to your timetable and writing regularly, the problem of picking up the threads and remembering where you had got up to when you are in the middle of a lengthy and complex piece of work can be challenging. If, however, you have stopped working on your thesis altogether for any period of time, the thought of picking up where you left off can seem almost impossible. At such a point, it is not unusual to feel really stuck, and unable to begin writing, or even reading, again. This sets off a downward spiral – the more disheartened you feel, the less you feel able to get yourself started. The more weeks that go by without your having written anything, the more disheartened you feel, and the more difficult it becomes to start writing again, and so on. Furthermore, whatever stage *you* are at, if others who began the programme at the same time as you have kept up with their work, they will be further ahead than you. Possibly, therefore, they will be less interested in studying and consulting with you than with others who have reached the same stage as they have. This might be especially true if you are working online. Discussions might have moved on to a new topic and course colleagues may have failed even to notice that you have disappeared from the discussion board. This can leave you feeling isolated and unsupported.

Reasons why students get behind: summary of key points

- An extension for one piece of work can easily lead to the build-up of a huge backlog.
- The feeling of being behind is disheartening. This can make it even harder to get going again, so a vicious circle of demotivation is created.
- After a break of more than a fortnight, it can be difficult to remember where you are up to and what you had been taught in relation to your assignment/thesis. The longer the break, the harder it becomes to pick up where you left off.
- The problems that prevented you from handing in work on time in the first place may still exist.
- If you are on a 'taught' programme, your peers will have moved ahead without you, which may leave you feeling lonely and unsupported.

Missed deadlines and coping with a muddle

This section provides suggestions about how to pick up your coursework and start writing again after a break – either planned, or as a result of having got behind. Before discussing writing techniques, however, I will tackle the practical issue of what to do when your work is in a muddle, when you are behind with your schedule and things are not going to plan. This can be a lonely and isolating position to be in but, for part-time learners especially, it is not uncommon. In this section I shall differentiate between problems which may be in their early stages and problems which might require some serious re-evaluation if you are to continue your course. I address the possibility of non-completion, and consider how this may be managed positively.

Personal problems and study

Sometimes, personal or work commitments 'get in the way' of part-time study. No matter what your age, or how well organized you are, the pressures of paid work and family may put so much pressure on you that part-time study becomes very difficult. This may require you to negotiate with your university/ college as well as with family and friends, or employers.

Potential problems

Let's start at the simplest end of the scale by looking at problems which are looming, and threaten to pose a problem, but have not actually done so yet. What if you know in advance that work, health or family issues are likely to interrupt your progress? When things are tough, probably the last thing you feel like doing is contacting someone at your institution, particularly if this means talking in cyberspace to someone you have never met about something which may be very personal. However, it is worthwhile giving this a try. This is because, despite the tendency for universities and colleges to treat all students in the same manner (see Chapter 1), they can, by contrast, be surprisingly understanding about genuine personal dilemmas and may be able to offer assistance if you are really struggling. So if you are facing real personal difficulties, which might affect your study, *don't try to hide these from your university*. Contact your tutor/supervisor as soon as possible, and see what help might be available. There are a number of possible options that might be on offer (though bear in mind that these will vary from place to place, and some institutions will be more accommodating than others).

You might, for example, find that you can suspend your studies for a period, or agree an extension on deadlines when work should be handed in. You may also find that your institution can be flexible about how you fulfil course requirements, as in Dan's example below. Bear in mind that you may have to provide some evidence of the reason why your circumstances are extenuating.

For example, if you want to defer your studies on health grounds, you will probably be required to produce a doctor's note. Gatrell and Turnbull (2003: 62) suggest ensuring that you obtain any agreements made between yourself and your institution in writing. This will protect you in an instance where, for example, you have come to an arrangement with an individual tutor/supervisor, or course manager, who then leaves, or who should not have made the arrangement in the first place. For example, supposing you decide to suspend your studies for a given period. In such circumstances you need to be assured of details such as: how long you can suspend your studies for; how you will be integrated back onto the course when you return; and, importantly, what your fee status will be on your return. It is also worth asking what will happen should you decide, in the end, that you do not wish to continue with your course. Will you be expected to pay any additional fees if you are unable to rejoin the programme and, if so, what will these be? And will you be disadvantaged should you wish to register for the same or another course at the same institution in the future?

Dan, in the example below, describes how he successfully negotiated an exemption from an overseas assignment. He managed this by explaining to his tutor/supervisor his circumstances well in advance of the module and by helping to sort out the arrangements himself.

Student experience

I got divorced and at the same time my elderly mother became ill. So I moved in with her and I ended up pretty tied, as a carer. I am an antique dealer and I had built up a lot of knowledge in my field. But I was not qualified; I had left school at 16. So I started a part-time degree in History of Art and they let me in without A-levels because I had the experience. They had modules which were supposed to be residential but since they were held in [city X], near my home and shop, I was able to attend them and return home each night and somehow I muddled through. In the final year of the programme, though, there was an overseas module, which was compulsory and involved a workplace project in a European art gallery. I had always known about this, but I suppose I had vaguely hoped that by the time I got to that point in the course my mother might be a bit better, or I would have sorted out alternative arrangements for her, or something. In the event, though, neither of these things had happened. I finally faced talking to my tutor, who was more sympathetic than I had thought she would be. Fortunately I had given her a reasonable amount of notice. She got permission for me to do this project in a local art gallery in the city where I lived. We had to go to a fair amount of trouble to set this up, but in the end it worked. So I was able to complete my degree and graduate.

(Dan, part-time undergraduate, History of Art)

Locking the door after the horse has bolted

Suggesting that you plan for disaster is all very well if the disaster hasn't yet occurred. But what can you do if you are already in a real mess with your work? How can you retrieve the situation if you are several assignments behind, or if your thesis was due in last week but you haven't actually started writing it yet? As noted earlier in this chapter, it is not unusual for part-time students to find themselves in this situation. This is partly because (depending on the type of programme you are doing) there may be fewer face-to-face meetings and deadlines involved, and consequently less opportunity for your institution to keep tabs on where you are up to (or to notice if you are falling behind). This is particularly likely to be the case for students learning online, who may disappear without trace before anyone has even noticed they are missing. As Gatrell and Turnbull (2003: 91) point out:

> It can be much more difficult for [part-time] students to motivate themselves when they do not have the discipline of regular face-to-face contact with their group and their tutors. The first thing that happens when students fall behind . . . is that they stop logging on to the conference site . . . [and] as time passes it becomes increasingly difficult to re-enter the discussion . . . it is much easier to avoid contact with your colleagues and tutors/supervisors when you are studying online than it is when you have to attend regular classes and this is a clear disadvantage.

Often, the reason for getting very behind in your work (as noted earlier) is because some slippage has occurred earlier on in the course, adding to the pressure you are already under and making it ever more difficult to catch up. The consequences of failing to hand in work on time are rather like the accumulation of financial debt – which has a habit of mounting up until it becomes unmanageable. If, for example, a person was supposed to repay the mortgage on their house at £1000 per calendar month, and they missed one payment due to financial pressures, they would owe £2000 the following month. Assuming that their financial circumstances had not changed, £2000 would be twice as difficult to deliver as £1000 and the debt would quickly spiral out of control and become impossible to pay off. At this point, the person's options would be: to ignore the problem; to borrow some more money from elsewhere (which in its turn would have to be paid back); or to contact the lending company and explain the problem. If the latter option is chosen, the person could request some arrangement which would allow them to get back on track with payments, such as paying back the missing amount over 12 months, or paying interest only for a period of time while they try to sell the property, or extending the life of the loan.

The case of the build-up of debt is a useful analogy, because none of the solutions are ideal, but the results of ignoring a build-up of debt are not dissimilar to those of ignoring a backlog of academic work – everything very quickly becomes overwhelming and unmanageable. The advice about coping with overdue academic work is similar to the advice given to those who are struggling with debt. The first step you need to take is to face up to the extent of the problem. Sit down with a piece of paper and produce a 'slippage' time-table. Write down exactly where you are now, in relation to where you should have been. Do this in some detail. If you have done some work on some of your assignments/project, include it, but don't exaggerate the extent of this. Your slippage timetable should look something like the example given below, in which Jane Smith has fallen behind in her Art History programme and is considering her options.

Example: slippage in study programme

Jane Smith, part-time degree in Art History
Course began: September 2006
Today's date: 15 December 2007

Essay title	Hand in date	Date submitted	Where up to
Gothic Art	December 2006	On time	Complete
Renaissance Art	March 2007	April 2007	Complete
Victorian Art	June 2007	Oct 2007	Complete
Impressionism	Sept 2007	Not submitted	Some reading/notes taken
Modern Art	December 2007	Not submitted	Nothing done
Dissertation	May 2008	Not due	Not started

Looking at the slippage in Jane Smith's imaginary programme, it is evident that the problems began in March 2007, when the essay on Renaissance Art was not completed on time. Since that date the slippage has got worse, and now Jane should be starting on her dissertation but still has two essays owing. For one of these, she has done some reading – though if she did this some weeks ago, she may need to refresh her memory about where she was up to, which takes time. What might Jane's options be, and what might she need to take into account?

Jane's first step would be to evaluate whether it is both worthwhile and feasible to continue with her course at this stage, or whether she has fallen so far behind that this has become impossible. In Jane's case, it is evident that she has already invested a substantial amount of time (and presumably money) in her programme, having handed three pieces of work in so far (albeit two of these late), and presumably paid fees during this period. Thus, if she wishes to make the most of her investment Jane will probably consider that it is worth her while to keep going. However, the feasibility element of the question sug-gests the need for some strategic action, which can only be determined in the context of a conversation with Jane's tutor/supervisor. Jane will need to nego-tiate some kind of extension or suspension of studies because otherwise, any hopes of catching up and finishing on time would seem to be unrealistic since this would involve completing two assignments and a dissertation in a six-month period. Thus, Jane will need to speak with her tutor/supervisor at the earliest opportunity to investigate what alternatives might be on offer. Jane may, for example, be able to work on the dissertation, aim to finish this on time and submit the two assignments subsequently. However, she would need to ensure that completion of a dissertation, without first having done the groundwork required for the final two assignments, was a sensible strategy. Alternatively, she might be able to suspend her studies and rejoin the course the following year in June 2007, at the point when work on the Impressionism assignment was due to begin.

If you are in a similar situation to Jane's, you will need to ascertain the rules and regulations about what you do before you make your decision. For example, what impact does the late submission of assignments have on marks? Some institutions will only award a basic pass for something which is late, even if the work is of a high standard. You will also need to be crystal clear about the fee situation. If you suspend your studies, does this mean that no fees will be due during the period of extension? Or will you be obliged to pay some kind of retainer? And will the suspension of studies mean that you are excluded from facilities such as online library provision, meaning that your opportunities for catching up with assignments while your registration is suspended are limited? If you have not already done so, it is essential that you get in touch with your tutor/supervisor since you cannot make these decisions without a discussion with her or him. If you are truthful about your reasons for lack of progress and you can provide a convincing argument for why your institution should offer you support, as well as a sensible timetable for making up lost ground, there is a possibility that your faculty will see what can be done to offer you support. If, on the other hand, your story seems implausible and you have no real plan of action for dealing with the slippage that has occurred, course staff might be less obliging. It usually helps if you can be straight-forward about your situation. Most tutors/supervisors are familiar with (and unsympathetic towards) stories about the cat knocking a mug of tea over the computer causing the loss of all your work, which had been written but not printed out. You may also find it difficult to persuade your tutor/supervisor that she or he should allow you to continue if you have a history of late submission and poor-quality work. If this is the case and you are determined to continue on your programme, the submission of a series of well-constructed and clearly thought-out assignment or essay *plans*, with appropriate timescales attached, might help your case. However, be prepared for some cynicism or lack of enthusiasm on your faculty's part.

Assuming that you have persuaded your tutor/supervisor and your institution to accommodate you, it is really important that you agree a timetable and stick to it. Picking up your studies after a break won't be easy, and anyone who has struggled with assignment or dissertation writing is likely to find it even harder to get going after a break than when they were managing to submit

academic work on time. This section is followed, therefore, by some suggestions about how you might pick up the threads of your coursework following a
break, focusing in particular on how to begin writing again. If you find, however, that even with extensions and suspensions you are still struggling to keep
up, this might be the moment to face up to the possibility that this is not the
right time, or the right part-time course, for you. You may have to accept that
you are not going to complete it. A discussion about pulling out takes place
below.

Giving up

For understandable reasons, most textbooks neglect to cover the challenges
faced by students who drop out of their degree courses. This is probably
because the majority of study guides focus on goals, achievement and successful completion, so failure to complete the course is not on the agenda.
Additionally, universities and colleges seek to present a positive image of
themselves and are unlikely to advertise low completion rates.

But this book would not be true to itself if it did not include this section. The
reason why it is important to consider 'giving up' is because, while institutions
might go to some trouble to keep 'under wraps' rates of non-completion on
part-time courses, these are often much higher than you might imagine. This
is especially likely to be the case where students are learning at a distance over
long periods of time. Thus, if you are at the point of giving up, it is important
to be aware that you are not alone. Although giving up is not what anyone
intends when they begin, there will be some students for whom continuing
their course is simply not an option. Often, this is not because students are not
enjoying their course (those who leave for that reason will probably make their
decision not to complete at an early stage). Nor is it because they are not bright
enough to meet the required standards. Often, non-completion occurs for one
or more of the following reasons.

Reasons for non-completion of part-time study: summary
of key points

- Life events have imposed so much pressure on part-time students that continuing is impossible.
- Students have underestimated the demands of combining part-time study
  with employment and/or caring work.

- Events have led to students falling behind, and catching up has become impossible.
- Students are no longer able to finance their studies – either because sponsors are no longer willing to pay or because self-funding students run into unanticipated financial difficulties.
- Students who are on a distance learning programme feel lonely and isolated in their study and this leads to demotivation and slippage in study schedules.
- Occasionally because students 'find the level of the course too high to be able to complete it' (Talbot 2003: 12).

Unsurprisingly, part-time students who do not complete their study programmes feel low, and downhearted. They may also feel quite isolated, especially if they have been studying at a distance and were already progressing their studies in a fairly lonely situation. Science and Technology student Katherine Sargant (2000) explains how a run of ill-health and the pressures of study combined with raising her infant son meant that she could no longer continue. Katherine recalls how circumstances combined and she finally reached the point where she was obliged to withdraw from her programme:

> October comes and I try to get back on the merry-go-round. This time, I believe I am going to balance the time better between study and family. I fail. We all get the usual October bug, and I can no longer hold my balance. We all battle on with the bug till December, then it's crunch time. No work completed, and my academic focus [has] all but disappeared.
>
> (Sargant 2000: 64)

Luke (who explains his circumstances below) was doing a part-time degree in Political Science over six years which involved part online and part face-to-face tuition. Luke got seriously behind with his work and was unable to catch up. He gained permission to suspend his studies for 12 months, but gradually recognized that picking up where he had left off was going to be very difficult because the circumstances which had contributed to his problems in the first place were still there. He held a demanding job (which was unconnected with, and did not require a degree in, Political Science) and had underestimated the amount of time that his part-time degree would require. Because of this underestimation, he had not had a chance to talk things through properly with his partner, who also worked and felt that Luke's studies placed an unreasonable burden on her in terms of the housework and childcare that she was expected to manage. Once behind with his assignments, Luke, who had always found writing to be difficult, felt that he could not catch up. At the end of his 12-month break he withdrew from his degree programme.

Student experience

I got a new job and for a few months I was just totally focused on that. I started by asking for an extension for one essay for six weeks, which I got, but even when I had a bit of spare time I just couldn't get down to writing. Before long I had also missed the deadline for the next essay and so I was two behind. At this point, the pressure was really starting to get to me. I have never found writing exactly easy but I was determined to get back to where I should be and carry on. So I took some holiday – a whole week. And my wife Janet was a bit resentful because she said, 'You are working all the time; you said you didn't have time to go away with me and the kids at half-term because you were so busy!' So I felt even more pressured to produce something decent during that week and to catch up with my work.

Well, Monday morning came and Janet went off to work and the kids to school and I sat there in front of the computer and I couldn't write anything. So I played some games online and tried again, but nothing. So I paced the floor and made coffee and by mid-afternoon I had still done nothing. So I rang work to see how things were going and then did some e-mails and before I knew it the whole day had gone by and I hadn't written anything. So on Tuesday I felt under even more pressure to produce something and in the end I washed and polished the car, which I would never do – I go to the car wash. And every night Janet said 'Well, how's it going then?' and I would say, 'Oh, fine.' And before I knew it, it was Friday. And on Friday I went into work, and they said 'How's your college stuff going?' and of course I said, 'Oh, fine.' And then on the Friday night Janet said, 'So let's see what you've written then.' And I got cross and said 'You're not the teacher; I don't have to answer to you. Don't treat me like a child.' But in the end I had to confess that I hadn't written anything, which I think she knew really. And she was not best pleased that I had wasted the week. And I'd like to say that I got a hold of it, but I just couldn't. I was facing the whole day with two essays to write and nothing written and I just couldn't write anything; the task was so huge I just didn't know where to begin.

(Luke, part-time undergraduate, Political Science)

Biting the bullet and withdrawing gracefully

Under circumstances like those of Luke and Katherine, the most sensible way forward is to take the decision yourself to withdraw from your programme of study. This is better than letting the situation get worse and worse, until you find yourself collapsing under a build-up of late assignments/research and guilt. Contact your tutor/supervisor, explain the situation and work out what you need to do in order to leave your institution on good terms. If you can be positive about particular aspects of the programme, then do so, and say 'thank you'. Unless you have a specific cause for complaint (in which case refer to the section on complaints later in this chapter), be prepared to take responsibility for your own decision not to continue, and be truthful about this.

If you are open with your tutor/supervisor, she or he is likely to be more sympathetic than if you try to 'cover up' your lack of progress, or if you are critical of her/him – especially if part of the problem lies at your door. Ending things on a good note with your tutor/supervisor is worthwhile. You might, at a later date, want to pick up your studies again either in your own institution or elsewhere and you might then seek a reference from your original adviser. Furthermore, although academic staff usually have little to do with the administration of course fees, your adviser might be in a position to make a case on your behalf to reduce or waive fees – especially if these relate to future study. (In relation to course fees, you must be prepared for the possibility that leaving a course part way through might mean paying for tuition at least up to the end of the academic year.) Although 'giving up' is never likely to be a happy experience, if you take control of the 'ending' you are likely to feel better than if you simply fail to turn in assignments/research work and disappear from view, meaning that your university will eventually deem you to have withdrawn from your programme. As a further incentive for creating closure, bear in mind that leaving your programme, rather than being pushed off it, might save you money, as you might be able to negotiate a reduction in fees relating to forthcoming tuition. I end this section with a comment from June, a lecturer on a part-time creative writing course.

The lecturer's view

I am a lecturer on a part-time degree course in creative writing. The course is modular and involves weekend work; they start on Friday morning and go home on a Sunday lunchtime. Students usually work closely in small learning groups and they have to prepare work in advance which they present as part of the module, then they work on it together. I put a lot of effort into the course (especially given it takes up my weekends) and I rely on the students to do their bit. Last year, I had a student called Patricia. It was January and she was a first-year student who had begun the course in October. Previously she had always turned up on time and had handed in the two required pieces of work. On the Friday morning when the module was due to start, she didn't turn up (and nor did her written assignment). We waited for her for a while then we began without her. It was a bit inconvenient because she was supposed to have prepared some work on behalf of her learning group, so they had to manage without her contribution as well as being one person down. Patricia did not call to say what had happened which I was a bit surprised about. We e-mailed her, and the other students left messages on her mobile but she didn't respond.

The following week, I wrote to her reminding her that the module was compulsory and asking her to get in touch. I eventually heard from her about two weeks later. She was very upset and told me that her husband had left her two days before the module was due to begin, which was why she had not attended. She had not phoned up because she had been too upset to talk. The two weeks had given Patricia time to think and even though I could have figured out a way for her to catch up with the course she did not feel that she wanted to do this. I was pleased that Patricia had contacted me in person because then I knew what the reason was. It wasn't something wrong about the course, or anything that had happened in her group. It also enabled me to make a case to the finance office on her behalf. In theory, she should have paid up until the end of the academic year because it was obviously too late to offer her place to someone else. But I explained the circumstances to the finance people and Patricia got a doctor's note. So they waived the fees for the Lent and Summer term, and took her off the books thereafter. I liked Patricia and I am glad she explained things to me because now I can happily give her a reference if ever she needs one for another course. I would be pleased to have her back on my course if ever she decided to give it another go.

Taking something with you

If you leave your part-time course before you reach the end of it, you will obviously, temporarily at least, be forgoing the qualification for which you were aiming. Usually, however, you can identify some positive things you have taken from the experience – perhaps the learning, or friendships with others on the course. Katherine Sargant, the part-time Technology student who gave up her studies following ill-health and family pressures, dealt with her decision to leave by focusing on the benefits she had gained from part-time study. Katherine appears to have left her university on good terms. She indicates that she might in time seek the funding to study full-time, and return. I shall end this section with Katherine's summary of the good things about part-time learning:

Giving up is never a failure. It is usually common sense coming into focus . . . I continue to tinker with various ideas, waiting for funding to fall into place. The most useful things I have extracted from my experience of being a part-time [student] are the 'human' effects. Discovering my own abilities is one thing. But understanding the importance of the people bound up in my life, especially in academia, has been essential. I'm also learning how important it is to remain part of other people's lives. Support comes from many diverse places and remaining receptive to this support is essential.

(Sargant 2000: 64)

Deciding not to complete: summary of key points

- Be truthful with yourself about the extent of the problem. Can you catch up on missed deadlines simply by putting a bit of extra work in, or do you need to seek support from your institution?
- Talk to your course tutor/supervisor. Let her/him give you advice about what help might be on offer.
- Make sure you have checked the rules and regulations. Is it worth your continuing if you will receive only a bare pass mark for assignments which are submitted late?
- Be realistic about what you agree to. If you have got behind due to work or family pressures, are these likely to be any less difficult at the point when you plan to pick up your work again?
- Make sure you are crystal clear about the fee situation. Will your fee be reduced if you suspend your studies? Or will you be expected to continue payment at the full rate?
- If you decide to give up, take control of the situation, end on good terms with your university and try to focus on the benefits of your learning experience.

Picking up the threads and getting back on course

I have just dealt with the 'worst case scenario' – deciding that it is no longer feasible to carry on studying part-time, and withdrawing from your programme. We will now look at the other side of the coin – deciding that, however difficult this may be, you want to continue, even if you have taken a break from study and/or got behind with your written work. In Chapter 2, I gave tips on staying on top of your work and ensuring that you do not get behind in the first place. However, this advice (while it may be useful once you have got going again) is not necessarily going to be very helpful when you are already behind. What follows is a series of suggestions aimed at helping you pick up the threads when academic work has become difficult – either because there has been some unplanned slippage in your timetable, or because you have made the decision to take time out from your studies and are finding it difficult to get started again. This section will also be useful to those who may be up-to-date with their studies but are feeling uninspired and fed up. The ideas on offer are drawn from a range of sources – some are my own and some are provided by others (both experts and students).

Reading

To get yourself back into the swing of things, you can begin by doing some reading, or by talking things through, online or in person, with one of your course colleagues. Depending upon how long it is since you last produced any work, you might begin by reading something that is familiar, or that you enjoyed (which might remind you of why you wanted to do the course in the first place). The most difficult aspect of picking up your work is likely to be starting to write.

Why do we find writing so difficult?

For part-time students who are finding it hard to begin writing, it might be interesting to consider that even great writers sometimes got 'stuck', and struggled to meet deadlines. I noted in Chapter 3 the experiences of Anton Chekhov, the great Russian dramatist and storyteller. Chekhov was a qualified doctor so his 'day job', as a young man, was medicine, and his early dramatic and fictional writing was produced on a part-time basis. From time to time medicine took priority over writing, which made it difficult for him to commit to deadlines. In 1886, Chekhov wrote to Aleksey Suvorin, the proprietor of the *New Times* newspaper, which had recently commissioned him to write stories. Chekhov agree to be a regular contributor, but only on the basis that Suvorin understood the pressures of Chekhov's medical work:

> I write comparatively little: no more than two or three brief stories a week. [Yes,] I can find the time to write for the *New Times* but I'm glad neverthe-less that you didn't make deadlines a condition for my being a contribu-tor. Deadlines lead to haste and the feeling of having a weight around your neck. Both of these together make it hard for me to work. For me person-ally a deadline is inconvenient . . . because I am a physician and I practise medicine. I can never guarantee that I won't be torn away from my desk.
>
> (Chekhov 1886, quoted in Callow 1998: 74)

Many of us would consider that producing two or three short stories each week was quite an achievement for a part-time writer and would hesitate to describe this as 'comparatively little'. However, it is worth knowing that, for seven years, from 1890, following a play which was badly received, Chekhov became very downhearted. For months, he was unable to write anything and focused instead on his medical career. He then abandoned dramatic writing almost completely for the following seven years (Callow 1998), moving on to other things while he regained his confidence.

The disadvantages of contemporary writing styles

It could be argued that writing was more difficult in Chekhov's day than it is now because Chekhov did not have the advantage of a keyboard and personal printer, or even a typewriter. However, it is also possible to look at this the other way around and to suggest that writing is more difficult now than it was in the past, simply because formal writing is something that we do much less of now than in the days before information technology, especially if it is some years since we left full-time education. The days when people corresponded by letter and passed the time keeping diaries or journals have almost disappeared.

See, for example, the text message below, which is taken from Allison Pearson's (2003) novel *I Don't Know How She Does It*. Pearson's story centres upon the experiences of Kate Reddy, a high-flying British banker who combines motherhood with a demanding career and international travel. Kate is always busy and relies on technology for fast and easy communication about the latest crises developing at home. As the drama of Kate's life unfolds, Pearson's novel is peppered with written correspondence between Kate and her nanny, Paula. In the following instance, Kate is in America on business and is horrified to learn, via a text message from Paula, that her daughter has been sent home from school with head lice, which Kate herself may have contracted.

Text message from Paula Potts to Kate Reddy:

'Emly sent hme frm skool with NITS. hole famly must be treatd. U2! Cheers paula'

The instantaneous text message from Paula to Kate looks rather different from the fictional letter written by Hilary Swallow to her husband Philip. Philip Swallow is the hero of David Lodge's novel *Changing Places*, which was written in 1975. In the following extract, Philip, a British academic, is on an exchange visit to an American university. He has to rely on the old-fashioned postal service in order to receive Hilary's correspondence regarding the latest predicament at home.

Dearest [Philip]
Many thanks for your airletter. We were all glad to hear that you had arrived safely, especially Matthew, who saw pictures of an air-crash in America and television and was convinced it was your plane . . .
. . . I'm afraid our washing machine is make a terrible grinding noise and the service man says the main bearing is going and it will cost £21 to repair. Is it worth it or shall I trade it in for a new one while it's still working? . . .
. . . Oh – before I forget – I've not been able to find *Let's Write a Novel*, either here or at the University. Though I couldn't make a really thorough search at the University because Mr Zapp is already occupying your room.

I can't say I took to him . . . he seems to be a silent and standoffish sort of
person . . .
. . . Love from all of us here,
Hilary

(Lodge 1978: 119–20)

I have included both the text and the letter to help illustrate how contemporary forms of communication do little to help us develop, and retain,
the kind of writing skills required for academic writing. Contemporary correspondence tends to be short, pithy, and immediate, and Paula's text to Kate
typifies the kind of language that many of us use in our everyday lives, in a
society reliant on e-mails and mobile phones. Messages go straight to the
point, and the language and grammar we use in text messages looks nothing
like the writing style which is required by most academic institutions for
assignments, dissertations and theses.

Thirty years ago, however, when David Lodge's novel was written, letter
writing – even between a couple who had been married for years – was a much
more formal process. The layout and presentation of Hilary's letter, with its
carefully constructed sentences, correctly spelled words and detailed descrip-
tions of broken washing machines and lost books, is a world away from the
language of text and e-mail. A letter such as Hilary's would have required time,
attention and careful crafting before it was ready to send – and it would probably have taken well over a week to reach its destination! Nevertheless, the
postal service would have been the only option available for those with limited
financial resources, because e-mail did not exist and telephone calls in those
days would have been prohibitively expensive. By contrast, Paula's text would
probably have taken less than a minute to write and would have reached Kate
in seconds. However, while Paula's text has nothing in common with the kind
of writing that is required by educational institutions for academic, assessed
work, Hilary's prose – because it is written in a conventional style – shares
features in common with academic work.

The point I am making here is that, for the majority of contemporary
women and men, formal writing skills may no longer be an everyday
requirement. Even in the workplace, where you may be obliged to
produce reports, 'executive statements', bullet points and shortened sentences (often e-mailed), or powerpoint slides, have tended to replace the old-
fashioned decorum of formal documents. Thus, once people have left formal
education, many stop writing in 'prose' altogether. Even when a written
response is required (such as a reply to an invitation, or to thank someone
for a birthday gift), it is easy to purchase, or run off on the computer,
generic cards with messages such as 'wedding acceptance' already printed. So
writing becomes less and less a part of our daily lives. This point is made by
Alex, a student doing a Management degree, who describes his experiences
below:

Student experience

Why do I find writing so hard? What is it about the task that I find so difficult and why is there such an aversion?

I don't know how I can answer these questions; at least, I probably do know but I just haven't got to the point where the reasons come naturally. But it's probably something to do with history. We all have experiences that shape us. Then again, it probably has something to do with context – where I am now and the constraints, self-imposed or otherwise, that are prevailing on me.

Let's start with history. I don't come from a family where writing is the norm. It was never really expected of me, except, of course, the 'thank yous' that were obligatory at birthday and Christmas. My family traditions are more practical: hands-on tasks from my father, and music from my mother. I suppose I was also never really encouraged to read, so the drive to exchange ideas through the written word never became a reality.

As I grew up, my skills developed more in arts, crafts and music. Mostly I became accomplished at performance, and this has lasted to the present day. I've never seen writing, at least until recently, as a form of performance, which of course it is!

The second area is context. One of the big barriers is fear and I can identify this feeling whenever I am in a situation where I need to write. There is an interaction with history, too, however, because there are times in my professional career when writing has been traumatic. I won't go into these here but I can see now how the situations I have been in over the years have set up a pattern of avoidance – the natural consequence of fear engendered by trauma. Maybe by writing I will lay some ghosts to rest.

Then there is another part of context. In my daily life I find it difficult creating the space where I can devote my exclusive energies to writing. I have little enough time to spend with my family and I feel guilty about the apparent selfishness of taking time out for something that is just, at least in the early stages, between me and the paper . . .

(Alex, part-time undergraduate, Management)

In his story, Alex's view accords with the suggestion that writing is a craft which, if it has not been a part of your cultural background, may not come easily. He also makes the observation that writing is an emotional experience and that he associates it with fear and 'trauma'. This is in keeping with Horseford's (2000) recollection of doing a masters in Education, after which 'the physical pain of the experience had to fade to some degree' before she could contemplate undertaking further part-time study.

Rowena Murray considers fear and guilt to be important components in creating 'writer's block' and argues that: 'perhaps guilt and writing are associated because we are endlessly positioned as "not quite there yet", not quite good enough . . . It can feel as if failure is almost part of the process: we have failed to "pass" every time we write' (Murray 2002: 165). Paul Boyle (2005) expresses a similar viewpoint. It is important to remember that even the best-known writers, like Chekhov, may find themselves unable to write or obliged to break off from writing at some point in their career.

Seeing writing as 'doing' thinking

In the previous chapter, I gave tips on staying on top of your work and ensuring that you do not get behind in the first place. However, this advice (while it may be useful once you have got going again) is not necessarily going to be very helpful when you are already in a muddle with your work. Often, 'writer's block' is synonymous with getting behind with academic work. The feeling of being under pressure and the build-up of a backlog can be paralysing and it is easy to get to the point where, even if you have identified and ring-fenced some time for catching up, you are so keyed up that you are unable to write anything – as in Luke's example, above.

What follows are a series of suggestions to help make writing easier whatever stage you have reached in your programme. Whether you are behind with your work, or up-to-date but just feeling uninspired and fed up, I offer some ideas – both my own and those of others – to explain why we find writing so hard. I then offer some suggestions to help get the creative juices flowing. Hopefully, by trying out some of the following exercises, you will find that you can get over the hurdle of 'writer's block' and get started again.

The prospect of producing an assignment or a thesis may seem daunting because, when you begin writing, your focus is on a finished piece of work and not on a developing essay or thesis. This is even more likely to be the case when you are behind with your work and trying to produce an assignment in, say, one week – when others, who were up-to-date with their work, had perhaps six weeks in which to produce this. Thus, one of the reasons you may feel 'blocked' is because you are missing out on the 'thinking' stage of writing by attempting to produce a polished piece of work from scratch. This is a bit like attempting, metaphorically, to jump to the bottom of a flight of stairs rather than taking things step by step. No wonder it feels daunting.

The advice of 'experts' on writing suggests that you should think of writing as part of the *process* of developing your ideas, not something you do only *after* you have thought great thoughts. It is recommended that you should not worry too much about the 'end product' but begin by taking your time and using writing 'just for the sake of sorting your ideas out' (Clark and Ivanic 1997: 113). Boyle (2005) points out that, while many 'argue that writing reflects thinking, [I believe that] writing *is* a form of thinking' (Boyle 2005: 304, original emphasis). Clark and Ivanic build on the idea that you think and write at the same time. They explain that the traditional model of 'linear writing', in which you 'plan out' your essay or dissertation and then write up your work according to the plan, is unhelpful to many students because this does not reflect the way in which many of us think, or speak. Clark and Ivanic suggest that it is helpful look at writing as 'a way of pinning thoughts down . . . so you can go back to [them], refine them, build on them, discard or develop them'.

Murray (2002) points out that each of us has our own writing styles, and suggests that, especially if we are 'stuck', we should work in the area with which we are least comfortable. Thus, 'planners' who are trying to make progress should attempt some generative, or free, writing in which they worry less about the overall shape of their work and just write down what comes into their head. Those to whom 'freewriting' comes naturally might find it helpful to set themselves specific goals so that they know what the content of their piece of work will be to the extent of planning what will go in each chapter, and how many words each section is likely to be (see Elizabeth's suggestions on page 79). Murray observes that many students persuade themselves that they cannot begin writing because they lack quality time, only to find that, when they do have 'chunks' of writing time available, they feel overwhelmed and miserable, or end up producing nothing. She suggests alternating writing in short bursts with writing in big chunks – a 'binge-and-snack' approach (Murray 2002: 170). Murray argues the need to break your overall writing goals down into 'a series of smaller, more defined tasks'. Thus, you avoid sitting down for three days with the daunting (and probably unachievable) aim of catching up on the last three assignments, or writing a whole dissertation. Instead, you set yourself specific and manageable objectives, that are 'do-able' in the time you have available. I have adapted Murray's example for our purposes. So, for example, if you were writing an assignment over three days you might decide upon the following writing goals:

Writing goals – doing one assignment

Next week I have three days in which I intend to complete one assignment on Information Technology and Primary Education.
For my assignment, I am going to evaluate the benefits of using the internet in primary school education.
I am going to write 2000 words.
I am going to work from 9.00 to 5.00 each day with one hour for lunch.

(Adapted from Murray 2002)

For those working on a thesis or project, you might choose one section and work on that. Be specific – you can only do so much in three days.

Goal setting and warm-up exercises

Academics who advise on writing are generally agreed that beginning to write 'cold' is not a good way to begin. Sitting in front of a blank screen faced with the prospect of writing a whole essay or thesis is unlikely to inspire you and more likely to make you freeze up. Delamont (1997) recommends beginning to write with a pen on a piece of paper which is neither clean nor blank. She finds it helpful to start writing on scrap paper or on a used envelope. Having sketched out her ideas, she can transfer these to the blank computer screen. This provides a useful starting point and she is able to begin writing in earnest. Murray, as noted in Chapter 3, suggests writing to 'prompts', recalling what you wrote about last time you were working on your assignment or thesis, followed by a brief discussion of what you plan to write about now.

Both Murray (2002) and Boyle (2005) advocate that you should aim to produce a specific (and realistic) number of words in a given period of time. Boyle recommends 'setting yourself daily word targets' (p. 304). Before you begin writing, however, Murray recommends taking this a step further and breaking down your daily writing goals into even smaller, and well defined chunks, so that they feel manageable. This will enable you to readjust the number of words you plan to write if you have set yourself an unmanageable daily goal. So, for instance, if you have a whole day free, you might set yourself a goal for the first hour which might look like this.

Writing goals – breaking the task down

9.00 am: write for five minutes to prompts.
9.10–10.10: Draft out the introduction to my assignment on the benefits of the internet in primary schools. Write 200 words. In this introductory section, I will explain to the examiner what I propose to cover in this assignment. I will provide some background and context (100 words) then explain that I intend to look at both the benefits *and* problems associated with primary school children using the internet (50 words). I will explain why I think it is important to consider both sides of this argument (50 words).
10.10–10.20: coffee!
10.20–10.30: Read though and decide what I am going to tackle at 11.00 am.
(Adapted from Murray 2002)

If you had managed to sketch out your introduction by 10.10, then you could set yourself a further goal of another 200 words by lunchtime. If, on the other hand, you had written only 160 words, you could reduce your hourly target to 150 words – or, if you had made more progress than you thought, aim to write 250 or 300 words in the hour before lunch.

Aiming for a first draft, not perfection

The drafting and redrafting of written work is commonplace among authors. *Very* few people are like Simenon – able to sit down and write a book from beginning to end in a fortnight! However, this is often hidden from view, because what you see when you read published work in books and journals is the *polished and finished piece*. The messiness of writing (and the lack of inspiration or writer's block which may have been experienced by the author) is hidden from the reader. All those who advise on writing techniques emphasize the importance of drafts. Paul Boyle (2005: 304) suggests that:

> If you find yourself suffering from writer's block it is probably because you are attempting to perfect the product too early. All writers suffer long periods of time agonising over the working of single sentences, but . . . the modification of material can occur at a later date; nothing needs to come out right the first time.

Clark and Ivanic (1997) suggest that you begin by getting a rough draft down on paper so that you have something in front of you to work with, rather than just a blank sheet, and start to build up your thoughts from there. The advantage of a draft – even a messy, unwieldy draft – is that you have something down on paper. You have begun to free up your 'blocked' writing ability and you can now work on the draft and polish it up so that you feel able to show it to others. Do not be afraid of sharing drafts of your work with course colleagues or with tutors/supervisors. The comments of others can be helpful in shaping your work – and people can only comment on your written work once you have written something!

I think I'm going to write myself an e-mail

Still feeling stuck? Once you begin to think about your next assignment, or where you are in your thesis, you can put your ideas in writing. To spur yourself on, Murray (2002: 80), as noted above, suggests writing to 'prompts' such as: 'What writing have I [already] done?' And 'What do I want to write about next?' Write a note to yourself explaining why you are behind and assessing where you had got up to. Remembering Delamont's (1997) advice about avoiding a blank computer screen or sheet of paper you could do this as an e-mail, or you could handwrite it on a piece of scrap paper that looks neither 'blank' nor 'clean'. Your note should set the context, in terms of your current position and how you got there. It should discuss the topic of your next assignment (or what you are going to tackle next in your thesis) and be specific about what you are going to start with and why. Your note or e-mail should be reasonably well structured and should be written in proper sentences like Hilary Swallow's letter to Philip, though the language does not need to be formal. Don't try to deal with the whole of your assignment/thesis – just tackle one particular section. Then think about what you will move on to do once the chosen section is finished. An example is given below, adapted from my own learning notes and based on my experience of picking up my thesis after a six-month break. It is important to consider that looking at the example in this book gives the impression that the notes were much neater and tidier than they really were. The printed text obscures the messiness that was there, because all my notes were scribbled on lined paper in a notepad. The example has been updated and adapted in order to show how using Murray's (2002) prompts can structure your thoughts:

Student experience: author's letter to herself, after a break, about the next section in own thesis

---

Thesis
I stopped working on this thesis after the birth of my second baby. I haven't looked at it since and I can't bear the thought of starting. I can't really even remember where I had got up to. I promised myself a six-month break, but now that is over.

What did I write about last time? Thinking back, the bit I was writing just before my daughter was born was about the impact on mothers' health of having a baby. Then I thought about what happens when mothers go back to work. They often feel guilty about leaving their children and they are criticized in the media. Working mothers don't get much help from employers when they go back to work – they are just supposed to 'get on with it'. But in spite of this, mothers are committed to their jobs. Working mothers who live with men are still mostly responsible for housework. This is a bone of contention between some couples.

What do I want to write about next? I don't really want to write about anything. I am fed up and I just wish this thesis was finished. But I also don't want it hanging over me, so suspending my studies is not an answer. So for the next section, I am going to concentrate on the stuff about co-habiting couples and how far they share childcare. I probably *ought* to start on the bit about Anthony Giddens' theory of Structuration because that is what is worrying me more. But I think that might put me off doing anything at all. So I'll start with a bit that I know I can do. I will talk about how much childcare fathers do, and how much is left to mothers. I need to bring in the work of Lewis (1986), Lupton and Barclay (1997) and Dienhart (1998), who all write about fatherhood. I will say that fathers still don't do much housework but that, when mothers go to work, they take on more childcare, which they often enjoy.

When I have done all that (!!) I might start on the Giddens piece. But if I still don't feel ready, I might do the section on research interviews instead.

(Prompts from Murray 2002)

Talking online

If your course involves an online element, you could begin writing by trying an e-mail conversation with one of your course colleagues, who will understand what it is you are trying to write about and might well also understand what it feels like to be unable to get down to writing an assignment, or to pick up the threads of a thesis. The online conversation might throw up some ideas, and you can cut and paste these into your document, which will give you a 'starting point'.

Talking instead of writing

What if you feel so bogged down that you really can't write anything at all? Students who find it really difficult to put words onto paper are often articulate in the classroom, and can *talk* about what they propose to write with greater ease than they can actually write it. If you are really stuck, then the thought of writing a letter, or writing to prompts, or any activity involving writing might still feel like putting yourself under more pressure than you can bear. In this case you could try recording yourself. You don't need top-notch technology – an old tape recorder or camcorder will do. Organize yourself some time and privacy then, as if you are talking to your course colleagues, or a friend, describe out loud why you have got behind/taken a break. Remember to use your prompts. Ask yourself: 'Where had I got up to? What am I stuck on?', then go on to talk about 'What do I plan to write about next in relation to my assignment/thesis?'

If you think you might find it easier to talk to a 'real' person, see if there is someone who will put these questions to you, and who will then listen to you and either record what you are saying, or take notes for you. Once you have something recorded, you can transcribe this onto paper, in sentences – and you will have the basis of a plan which will help you pick up your assignment or thesis where you left off.

Making a habit of writing

In Chapter 3, I suggested that you should work towards getting into the habit of writing regularly. For readers who have got stuck, or behind with their writing, this is essential. Once you have pulled yourself out of the mire of extensions and late work, you do not want to find yourself bogged down again. Establishing a writing routine and sticking to it is therefore essential – see pages 90–92 for some ideas.

Picking up the threads and starting to write again: summary of key points

- Begin by reading and sketching out ideas on scrap paper rather than a clean sheet or a blank computer screen.

- Think of writing as a form of thinking and aim for a first draft, not perfection.
- Set yourself some writing goals.
- Write an e-mail to yourself, outlining the next stage in your assignment.
- If you can't write at all, record your thoughts and then transcribe them.
- Once you have got going again, establish a routine.

What to do when things go wrong

So far in this section I have focused on how you might retrieve the situation when you have fallen behind with your work and, in particular, what to do if you are struggling with writer's block.

What about when things go wrong and you feel that your university shares some or all of the responsibility for this? When is it appropriate to complain, and what can or should you do if you feel you are being unfairly treated by university staff, other students or both? Of course, this book cannot solve your problems for you, but it offers some examples of the difficulties which are sometimes faced by students and which are often not talked about in general conversation, course handbooks or study guides, meaning that those involved may feel isolated and unsure what to do. In what follows, I consider the delicate issues of intimate relationships between students and faculty, sexual and other forms of harassment, and make some suggestions about what you might do if you feel you have a grievance or complaint.

Intimate relationships between students and tutors/supervisors

> The degree of personal friendship [between students and tutors/supervisors] varies enormously. Some supervisors keep their students at arm's length and restrict themselves to formal relationships. Others enjoy and encourage greater degrees of friendship . . . That brings us to one potentially delicate [issue]: sex and the supervisor. It arises in a minority of cases but it does arise nevertheless . . . There is a power dimension to supervision which complicates the idea of any consensual sexual relationship between student and supervisor, whether gay or straight.
>
> (Delamont *et al.* 1997: 33)

The issue of sex and study can cloud relationships between students and tutors/supervisors regardless of whether students are full-time or part-time. However, in some ways it may be easier to fall into a relationship with your tutor/supervisor as a part-time student than if you are at university full-time. This is because, if you are a part-time 'present' student you may be resident on campus for intensive periods, perhaps involving evening teaching and social activities mixed with tutorial or supervision sessions on a one-to-one basis. Alternatively you may be a part-time student who meets your tutor/supervisor at venues outside office hours – and therefore outside the university setting, such as pubs or hotels. The duration of part-time programmes of study may be longer than those of full-time programmes and – especially if you are a research student – you might spend long periods in discussion with your tutor/ supervisor over a number of years. Inevitably, you will have at least some academic interests in common! These might be things that neither of you are able to discuss with friends or partners, since they relate to your own area of study and may not be shared by others. When meetings take place outside 'office' hours the formal discussions may drift naturally into social activities – drinks, or dinner. In these circumstances there is a possibility that some students and tutors/supervisors may find themselves becoming closely involved. The forming of a close relationship while one person is also marking the other's work can put both parties in a difficult position. Things might be especially problematic if the relationship breaks down, or if other students become aware of it.

Although this may not be stated in your course handbook, your university is unlikely to encourage relationships between students and tutors/supervisors, even if both parties are single and of similar ages. This is because while, generally, universities would not deem it appropriate to question the consensual sex lives of faculty and students, *once the two become academically linked there is a conflict of interest which the university would consider legitimated, and necessitated, institutional involvement.* Some institutions, such as Ohio and Duke University (in the USA), have established detailed policies which state clearly that faculty members should not enter into consensual relationships with students whom they are supervising. At Ohio University, there are severe penalties for faculty who continue to supervise students with whom they have become involved (Fogg and Walsh 2002). This followed on from bad publicity over a case where a 59-year-old, married male professor had had a relationship with a 23-year-old student, this resulting in unhappiness on both sides. Faculty members at Ohio are now 'prohibited' from intimate involvement with students whom they are supervising, and are obliged to report any such relationship to department heads. At Ohio, if students or faculty become intimate, the professor and the student concerned are encouraged to undergo counselling and to consider issues of harassment and exploitation, especially if they plan to continue the relationship. Failure on the part of the professor to report the situation could result in blocked promotion, suspension without pay, or even sacking.

In the case of Duke University, the policies are advisory and there are no penalties attached. Thus, there are no formal punishments for staff who contravene the policies. Nevertheless, the message is clear and staff at Duke are discouraged from becoming involved with students whom they are supervising; one gets the impression that senior personnel at Duke would not be supportive of staff who sleep with their students but then fail to withdraw from the supervisory role, as required by the policy. Whether or not your organization has a formal policy about relationships between students and tutors/supervisors, these can lead to academic complications and/or conflicts of interest. The *best option in all cases* is for the student to transfer to a different tutor/supervisor. As Delamont *et al.* (1997: 33) suggest:

> The guidelines for doctors and patients are a useful model for supervisors who feel an intimate relationship developing . . . if a sexual relationship develops, the student ought to have another supervisor.

In theory, should you find yourself in this difficult situation, your tutor/supervisor should take responsibility once your relationship has crossed the boundary between academic discussion and something more personal. There may, of course, be all sorts of reasons why she or he is reluctant to do this. Reporting mechanisms usually involve the head of department and your supervisor may fear the disapproval of colleagues. Additionally, there may be serious implications for others involved if either of you is in an existing partnership. Nevertheless, it is important that you address the conflict between your personal and your academic relationship, and if your tutor/supervisor has not already volunteered to do this, you need to talk through with her/him the necessity of taking some action, which should result in your transfer to an alternative tutor/supervisor.

Sexual (and other kinds of) harassment

Much of the research on sexual harassment focuses on the harassment of female students by male professors. There is often an assumption that harassment is something that mainly affects young women, who may have problems with the unwanted attentions of older male faculty. It has even been argued (by Frank Vinik, a lawyer at United Educators, which deals with American institutions) that there are occasional circumstances where male faculty regard opportunities to establish relationships with young female students as a 'perk' of their job (Fogg and Walsh 2002).

It is fairly well established that women are more likely to be the victims of sexual harassment than are men (Hatt *et al.* 1999). Nevertheless, harassment can take several forms, and some of the assumptions about its nature may be challenged. For one thing, women do not need to be young to experience sexual harassment – it may happen to mature female students, given the strong power dynamic involved in the relationship between students and their tutor/supervisor. Furthermore, harassment and other problems may occur between students, as well as between students and tutors/supervisors, as described in Jenna's example on page 65. Harassment is not exclusive to heterosexual relationships, and it may happen to men as well as women. DuLong (2004) observes that in the USA the number of sexual harassment claims filed by men has risen sharply over the past ten years. She further notes that sexual harassment may involve the use of homophobic behaviour to stigmatize those who do not meet gender stereotypes as far as their behaviour or dress is concerned.

What can you do if you consider that you are being sexually harassed? While not all institutions have formal policies relating to consensual sex between students and tutors/supervisors, most will have 'recognized procedures' for dealing with incidents of sexual harassment (Hatt *et al.* 1999). Once you have familiarized yourself with these, you can decide what is the best option for you.

If you have been upset by the behaviour of another student or students, or by a member of faculty, for other reasons (perhaps you believe you are being bullied or discriminated against on grounds of your ethnicity, gender, sexual orientation or any disability you may have), there will probably be university procedures in place advising you on how to deal with this. Look at your university website and see if there may be a harassment or equal opportunities officer from whom you can seek advice. And don't forget that, even though you are a part-time student, you can always turn to the student union for help. Part-time students (and especially mature students) tend to discount the student union, assuming it is there primarily for young, full-time undergraduates. However, the union is there to consider the needs of all students and it will usually, also, have established policies stating how it expects students to be treated, and to treat one another. If you feel you need support from people who understand universities, but you don't want to talk to faculty (at least in the first instance), then the student union should be able to offer you both information and support, and would be a good place to start.

Complaining about your university or your course

What if you decide that you have reason to complain about your university or course, for reasons other than, or in addition to, harassment? Once again, there will usually be a complaints procedure in place, but there may be things you can do to address the issues you are facing before you resort to formal procedures. Before going on to consider how, and in what circumstances, you might wish to complain, it is worth exploring why complaints might be an issue, particularly for part-time students. Arguably, there are some circumstances where part-timers feel that they have been disadvantaged in comparison with full-timers, even if this was unintentional on the part of the university. Perhaps this is more likely to occur in situations where procedures are set up principally to accommodate full-time needs, and may be less likely to be a problem in institutions like the Open University, which are set up especially for part-time study. Before you take the step of complaining, it is worth thinking about whether there may be a member of faculty or administration you know, and with whom you could talk the matter through informally before you make things 'official'.

Problems with your tutor/supervisor

If the problem is with your tutor/supervisor it might be worth sitting down with him or her face-to-face (or telephoning if this is not possible) and trying *tactfully* to explain what is worrying you. If you decide to correspond by e-mail, or if e-mail is your only option, *avoid the temptation to 'shoot off' a missive which seems angry or possibly discourteous.* Try typing out your concerns on a 'new document' first. Sleep on it and reread it (and/or get someone else to read it) before you send it off. Ensure that it gets your point across politely and succinctly, and that it offers the tutor/supervisor the chance to have his or her say. Be sure, too, that written correspondence expressing unhappiness does not come across as intimidating in tone. Occasionally, letters from anxious or dissatisfied students include threats to write to the Vice-Chancellor or Head of Department. These will do nothing to improve the situation, though they may cause the tutor/supervisor to withdraw altogether from supervising the unhappy student. Such warnings are usually unnecessary in any case – your institution will undoubtedly have a formal complaints procedure for you to follow, which should be available in your course handbook or on the university website.

Before dealing with matters by yourself, you may also want to check out whether you are a lone voice or whether others are affected. If so, they might support you, as in Bonnie's case, below. In Bonnie's situation, the grounds for complaint were fairly clear – the university had forgotten that the part-time pharmacy students had not covered the same things as the full-timers, so the part-timers had been disadvantaged in an important exam. Bonnie gathered the support of her fellow students and put their concerns down in writing.

Student experience

I was a part-time student doing a masters in Clinical Pharmacy. The way our part-time course ran, most of us were employed full-time but given a two-day release each week to attend modules at the university in the next town. We soon realized that our course was basically just part of the full-time programme. They did four days per week and we had a lot of extra reading, so it was very hard work. When it came to the exams, I sat down and looked at the paper and I realized that there was a question that I simply could not do – it was a topic that we had never covered. It occurred to me that this might have been taught to the full-time students, but not to us part-timers. As soon as the exam was over I checked this out and found I was correct. We got together as a group and composed a letter to the university. We did this right away, so that the papers would not have been marked. The university acknowledged what had happened and they compensated when they marked the part-time papers. They must have taken us seriously, and the compensation must have been about right because we all achieved the kind of marks we might have expected, and we all got through.

(Bonnie, part-time postgraduate, Clinical Pharmacy)

When things go wrong: summary of key points

- Intimate relationships between students and supervisors/tutors are not a good idea. They blur the boundaries of the academic relationship between the two parties, and if no action is taken, tutors/supervisors may attract the disapproval of their employing institution. If you find yourself in this situation, both of you need to take responsibility for ensuring your transfer to a different tutor/supervisor.
- Sexual and other forms of harassment are unacceptable in a university setting and most institutions will have policies in place to prevent this. If you feel you are being harassed, check out your university website, and find out what procedures are in place to help you deal with this. Remember that the student union should be there not only for full-time students, but also for part-time mature students. The union can provide an excellent source of support and advice.
- If you decide to complain about your university, do so only after you have thought out what you intend to say. See if you can sort things out informally first and, if not, check out procedures before taking action. If you decide to write, avoid dashing off a hastily composed e-mail but allow yourself time to think through what you intend to say.

7

What next?

At last, it had happened. After six years of study, I'd now got my degree. It was a very strange feeling, as during my studies I couldn't imagine actually getting to this point, but here I was. Most of the time I just concentrated on [whichever] course I was doing at the time, but sometimes I'd day-dream about getting to the end. But it always seemed so far off . . . The real landmark for me was the degree ceremony. This was the point at which I realized that I had finally reached my goal and the journey was over. It was also at this point that I discovered that, now I had finished the degree, I had a hole in my life. Clearly, I couldn't give up studying just yet . . .
(Open University graduate Stephen Collis, Open University 2004a: 20)

This chapter deals with the end of your part-time study. Drawing on student experiences, I discuss the issue of 'what next?' – what do you do after you have finished your part-time degree and how do you decide whether to continue? For some students, the completion of their part-time study is an end point. There is a sense of achievement, and of completion, and of delight that they have finished.

Student experience

Undertaking a part-time MPhil was a very challenging and difficult task. I had previously done a full-time masters degree and I found the difference between full-time study and part-time study challenging and hard to adapt to at first. The MPhil put pressure on my job and in particular on family life, which had to stop for many weekends, especially as the research phase of the course kicked in.

Completing and getting through the viva was a cause for real celebration and left a great feeling of accomplishment. My wife was particularly pleased – it meant I was able to get on with the ever-increasing list of jobs she had been saving up for three years!

(Joseph, part-time MPhil, Philosophy)

However, this is not the case for all. The point made by Stephen Collis, above, is not uncommon among part-time students. At the beginning and during the middle of their study, part-timers often feel (like Joseph) that they cannot *wait* to finish. But as their course draws to a close many feel – as Joanna did, in Chapter 1 – unable to give up part-time study because they have become 'addicted'. They no longer want the part-time study experience to end, and as they reach the final hurdle, their sights are set firmly on the next goal. This was certainly the case for me. Having undertaken a certificate in NHS Management, I was keen to gain an MBA. And as I progressed my MBA studies, and realized that a Distinction was within my grasp, I began to see the possibilities of doing a PhD. When I finished the PhD, there was no sense of loss such as that experienced by James, below. But the 'space' taken up by my PhD was rapidly filled by writing of other kinds – in particular, by the 'book' of the PhD – *Hard Labour: The Sociology of Parenthood* (Gatrell 2005) – and, of course, *Managing Part-time Study*.

Carrying on with part-time study, however, is not an easy decision to make. Inevitably, it will have implications for your finances and may mean (yet more!) understanding on the part of family, friends and colleagues.

Doing a PhD part-time

This is particularly pertinent if you decide you are going to undertake a PhD – the logical 'next step' for readers who have just finished a part-time masters programme, or who have gained a first-class honours degree in their undergraduate study. There is a huge difference between undertaking PhD study and either undergraduate, or masters level, part-time study. An undergraduate degree may take up to six years – around the same length of time it takes to do a part-time PhD – and a masters degree may take between two and five years, and will involve doing your own literature searches and a good deal of independent reading.

Nevertheless, doing a PhD part-time is more demanding than an undergraduate or a Masters degree. It is important to think hard in advance about what this entails. Part-time PhD study involves sustaining your motivation over a long period. Although you will have a tutor/supervisor who can provide regular advice and support, you will have to set your own deadlines, create your own research design and make other, important decisions about what to do, and how and when to do it, by yourself. On the other hand, although you will be in the driving seat, your work will probably be reviewed by your faculty every 15–18 months (every 12 months for full-time students) and even the most helpful and constructive reviews usually involve challenging the direction in which you are heading, and often a good deal of extra study and research. For a number of years, every time you think you are near the top of the mountain you will find that you have further to climb than you had imagined. Once you have gained your PhD, it is certainly worth it – but there are no guarantees and, as noted earlier, many of those who begin a part-time PhD fail ever to complete it.

So before you register for your PhD, it is worth giving the matter some serious thought. Ask your tutor or supervisor to give you an honest opinion about whether you should 'go for it', and really listen to what they say – even if it may not be what you hoped to hear. Ask yourself whether you are *sure* that you have the stamina and financial resources for what may be another five to seven years of part-time study? And ask yourself why you want a PhD. Simply for the title Doctor, which is very nice to have, but which may not be enough to sustain you over several years?

You will need a research topic that 'burns you up' and around two to three days each week to devote to your study – which is possibly a good deal more than you needed for your masters or undergraduate degree. To give you an idea of how I felt about this as a part-time PhD student, I quote below an extract from a short chapter I wrote during my second year of part-time PhD study. It is worth noting that, on average, I devoted three days per week to my PhD. I finished it within four years, but I was clear about my research topic at an early stage, and I had secured funding not only for course fees, but also for travel and other research costs. For some students (myself and Jack, whose experience is included at the end of this chapter), it helps to take some time out in between courses. In this way, you can spend some time recovering and devote yourself to other people and things. You can still use the time to take stock, and to do a bit of introductory reading for the next stage of your student career. It is probably worth trying to limit your break to no more than one year – it takes a long time to get into the 'habit' of part-time study, with the planning and discipline that this involves. If much more than a year passes, you might risk losing this precious habit, which has taken a long time to build up and might be very hard to recapture, once lost.

Student experience

When I registered as a PhD student, I was more complacent than I might have been about combining study with motherhood and employment. I had already completed a part-time MBA and gained a distinction. I assumed that this would prove to be an advantage – and in many ways it provided a good foundation [for PhD study] . . . I discovered that the discipline imposed by the MBA deadlines had become a habit, and the concept of late-night study was so familiar that this had become routine. The MBA had honed my writing and research skills and hugely improved my reading speeds. Nevertheless, there have still been aspects of PhD study for which I was not prepared.

Doing a PhD is completely different from working through a taught degree programme. Defined 'stepping stones' are laid out in the latter for you to follow and you can undertake your journey with focus and direction provided at each stage [by faculty], at least until you reach the point of doing the dissertation. Of course, the flexibility of doing a PhD can be advantageous for part-time students . . . as it gives you the valuable option of putting your research 'on hold'. You can return to it at a later date without having missed important coursework and without feeling behind in comparison with colleagues.

However, tackling a major piece of research, for which you are solely responsible, is intimidating. On beginning my PhD I felt daunted by the sheer scale of the work I was undertaking. . .Where should I begin? How would I know when I had done enough? And how would I ever settle on a suitable research question?

(Author, part-time PhD, Management)

(Gatrell 2000: 87)

Finishing part-time study and experiencing a sense of loss

For some students, the end of part-time study triggers unexpected emotional reactions. It is not uncommon to be left with a sense of loss, or even depression, which might last for some time. This can be difficult to handle as others will expect you to be jubilant, and in the mood for celebration. This feeling might happen even if you plan to continue your studies, and is something which is experienced by some famous writers. A biography of William Faulkner describes how this well-known writer himself recognized the pattern of excitement and achievement that accompanied finishing each book, which would inevitably be followed by a feeling of depression, and a fear that his creative abilities might fail him the next time. Faulkner's biographer, Bloom, writes:

Having finished the [final] revisions [of his latest book], Faulkner dated his typescript New York NY/October 1928 – and gave it to [his editor] Ben Wasson. It had been a long, intense and satisfying labor. 'I had just written my guts into the *The Sound and the Fury*', Faulkner said later. At first he felt exultant: 'Read this Buddy', he said to Ben Wasson. 'It's a real son-of-a-bitch.' But [Faulkner] had learned, years before, that for him the sense of completion often triggered depression and lifelessness, regret and guilt, and that, tomorrow, he was likely to 'wake up feeling rotten . . .'

The end he had laboured so hard to reach, he had also dreaded, as though he had not dared risk cutting off the supply [of inspiration], destroying the source [of his creativity].

(Bloom 1986: 185)

For those who have completed an undergraduate or a masters qualification, there is at least the prospect of the 'next stage', should you wish to continue. The deep sense of loss and depression on completing part-time study can be particularly acute for those who have submitted their PhD thesis, perhaps because submission follows such a period of intense labour (so, apart from anything else, you are likely to be overtired) and also because, once you have completed your PhD, you have gone as far down the road of part-time study as you can go. I remember handing in my thesis at the same time as a fellow student and each of us experiencing quite different reactions – mine was one of delight, but my friend experienced shock and emotional upset. Murray (2002) observes that these feelings may not be limited to the submission of your thesis, but that they may occur post-viva – even if things have gone well. Feelings might range from a sense of 'feeling a bit flat', as in Sophie's case below, to feeling a deep sense of loss, as in James's case. Murray attributes the post-viva blues to the fact that you have lost a key focus in your life and that the viva itself may have been difficult or disappointing in some way. The feelings of loss, and 'flatness', are described by James and Sophie, below.

Student experience

My viva was quite difficult, very tricky, and the examiners made little effort to be friendly or helpful. Nevertheless, I passed, and should in theory have been jumping for joy – it was over! But that didn't happen immediately. Instead, I was left with a sense of anti-climax – of feeling very flat. I remember some friends came over that evening and wanted to celebrate, and perhaps it was hard for them, and also for my partner, to understand that I wasn't really in the mood. I think one reason for this was that my own success – completing and passing my PhD – hadn't really sunk in. I had worked so hard and for so long that I couldn't really believe that I was there – I had done it.

(Sophie, part-time PhD, Educational Research)

I really prepared for my viva. Fortunately, I had had a mock, which had not gone to plan. So after that I spent a good deal of time planning and revising in order that I could give a good account of myself at the viva. The hard work paid off and the viva went well. I went into the room Mr, and came out Dr. It should have felt fantastic.

I was unprepared, however, for the feelings I experienced on learning that I had gained my PhD. I had expected to be overjoyed, but that didn't happen. Instead, immediately afterwards, I felt a sense of loss, and of shock. This lasted for days – even weeks – after the event. Following the viva, I rang my partner to let her know I had passed. Obviously, she wanted to know all about it, but I just couldn't bear to talk about it – either on the phone or when I got home. I felt bad about this, as she had been so supportive for so long, but I just couldn't get the words out. It wasn't really until several weeks later, when I agreed to give a talk to a group of students who were at the viva stage, that I was able to revisit the event in my mind. I have just about recovered, now, from this sense of loss. But for ages it felt as though there was something missing from my life – almost as if I was in mourning.

(James, part-time PhD, Management)

Be aware that these feelings are usually temporary – and that you can always progress to the next stage and seek to publish your research in some form, if you have not done so already. Even if you are not planning to join the academic community (a new lecturer's pay may not be sufficiently tempting, especially if you already hold a senior job), you can still work towards ensuring that your contribution to knowledge makes it into print. Your PhD supervisor and/or your external examiner should be pleased to help in this regard, so once you have had time to catch your breath, and recover from the PhD experience, this might be the next route to take. For those of you who are thinking of continuing from undergraduate to masters level, or from masters to PhD level, only you can make the decision about 'what next'. You are, at any rate, in a good position to think things through, since you already know many of the difficulties involved. As I close this book, I wish you all the best with your part-time study, and I will give the last words to Jack, the part-time student who graduated with an MBA, and who is now on the road to attaining his part-time PhD:

Student experience

Soon after starting my MBA, it was obvious to me that I wanted to study beyond the MBA. The MBA had really ignited a learning passion, but an MBA is a very structured study programme. So just as I started to delve into an area that I was passionate about, it was time to move on and really, that's when the scene for a PhD was set.

However, whilst my wife appreciated my desire to learn, and accepted the career benefits that a doctoral degree would bring, she was very conscious of the impact that study has on family. So she asked me to agree to a simple condition – no study, at all, for two years after the MBA. This was very wise; much wiser than I appreciated at the time. Not only did this break ensure that I took time out from study to spend with my family – but it meant that I had to take time to reflect on my future. A very wise move, in retrospect. So after two years, I started to investigate a PhD. The original condition, of course, was 'no study' for two years. I respected the meaning of this and so I didn't investigate PhD study options during this time either. But that burning desire to learn more didn't go away. Before I knew it, the two years was over, I was registered as a PhD student and we were back to lost weekends and family apologies for spending time with books and not children.

Easy, no. Hard, absolutely.

Worth it? Ask me in another three years.

(Jack, part-time postgraduate, MBA and now registered for a PhD)

References

Assouline, P. (1997) *Simenon: A Biography*, translated from the French by Jon Rothschild. London: Chatto and Windus.

Auger, V. and Overby, L. (2005) Teaching and learning in Nanjing: community, communities and politics in an overseas program, *Journal of Political Science and Education*, 1(2): 233–47.

Bloom, H. (1986) *Modern Critical Views: William Faulkner*. New York: Chelsea House Publishers.

Booth, W.C., Colomb, G.G. and Williams, J.M. (1995) *The Craft of Research*. London: The University of Chicago Press.

Boyle, P. (2005) 'Writing the report' in R. Flowerdew and D. Martin (eds) *Methods in Human Geography: A Guide for Students Doing a Research Project*. Harlow: Pearson/Prentice-Hall.

Callow, P. (1998) *Chekhov: The Hidden Ground*. London: Constable.

Chan, S. (1999) The Chinese learner: a question of style, *Education and Training*, 41(6–7): 29–30.

Clerk, R. and Ivanic, R. (1997) *The Politics of Writing*. London: Routledge.

Collinson, D. and Collinson, M. (2004) The power of time: leadership, management and gender, in C.F. Epstein and A.L. Kalleberg (eds) *Fighting for Time: Shifting the Boundaries of Work and Social Life*. New York: Russell Sage Foundation.

Curry, M.J. (2003) Skills, access and 'basic writing'. A community college case study from the United States, *Studies in the Education of Adults*, 35(1): 5–18.

Delamont, S., Atkinson, P. and Parry, O. (1997) *Supervising the PhD: A Guide to Success*. Buckingham: Open University Press.

De Verthelyi, R.F. (1995) International students' spouses: invisible sojourners in the culture shock literature, *International Journal of Intercultural Relations*, 19(3): 387–411.

Dienhart, A. (1998) *Reshaping Fatherhood: The Social Construction of Shared Parenting*. Thousand Oaks, CA: Sage Publications.

Dodds, A. (2000) To PhD or not to PhD?, in N. Greenfield (ed.) *How I Got My Postgraduate Degree Part-time*. Lancaster: Independent Studies Series.

DuLong, J. (2004) Challenging masculinity, *Advocate*, Vol. 925: 15.

Flowerdew, R. and Martin D. (eds) (2005) *Methods in Human Geography: A Guide for Students Doing a Research Project*. Harlow: Pearson/Prentice-Hall.

Fogg, P. and Walsh, S. (2002) The question of sex between professor and students, *Chronicle of Higher Education*, 48(30): 8–9.

Gatrell, A.C. and Flowerdew, R. (2005) Choosing a topic, in R. Flowerdew and D. Martin (eds) *Methods in Human Geography: A Guide for Students Doing a Research Project*. Harlow: Pearson/Prentice-Hall.

Gatrell, C. (2000) Mission impossible: doing a part-time PhD (or getting 200% out of 20% – is it really worth it?), in N. Greenfield (ed.) *How I Got My Postgraduate Degree Part-time*. Lancaster: Independent Studies Series.

Gatrell, C. (2005) *Hard Labour: The Sociology of Parenthood*. Maidenhead: Open University Press.

Gatrell, C. and Turnbull, S. (2003) *Your MBA with Distinction: Developing a Systematic Approach to Succeeding in your Business Degree*. Harlow: Financial Times/Prentice-Hall.

Giles, K. and Hedge, N. (2002) *The Manager's Good Study Guide*. Milton Keynes: Open University Press.

Habu, T. (2000) The irony of globalization: the experience of Japanese women in British higher education, *Higher Education*, 39(1): 43–66.

Hakim, C. (2000) *Work–Lifestyle Choices in the 21st Century: Preference Theory*. Oxford: Oxford University Press.

Hashim, I.H. and Zhiliang, Y. (2003) Cultural and gender difference in perceiving stressors: a cross-cultural investigation of African and western students in Chinese colleges, *Stress and Health*, 19(4): 217–25.

Hatt, S., Kent, J. and Britton, C. (1999) *Women, Research and Career*. Basingstoke: Macmillan.

Hendry, C. and Farley, A. (2004) Making the most of time, *Nurse Researcher*, 12(2): 81–9.

Hochschild, A. (1997) *The Time Bind: When Work Becomes Home and Home Becomes Work*. New York: Henry Holt.

Holtham, S. (2000) The agony and ecstasy of part-time study, in N. Greenfield (ed.) *How I Got My Postgraduate Degree Part-time*. Lancaster: Independent Studies Series.

Horseford, A. (2000) Long distance relationships, in N. Greenfield (ed.) *How I Got My Postgraduate Degree Part-time*. Lancaster: Independent Studies Series.

Hughes, B. (2005) Study, examinations and stress: blood pressure assessments in college students, *Educational Review*, 57(1): 21–36.

Kember, D., Chan Kwok Ying, Chan Shun Wan *et al.* (2005) How students cope with part-time study: an analysis of coping mechanisms through an on-line forum, *Active Learning in Higher Education*, 6(3): 230–42.

Leask, B. (2006) Plagiarism, cultural diversity and metaphor: implications for academic staff development, *Assessment and Evaluation in Higher Education*, 31(2): 183–99.

Le Ha, Phavi (2006) Plagiarism and overseas students: stereotypes again?, *English Language Teachers Journal*, 60(1): 76–8.

Lewis, C. (1986) *Becoming a Father*. Milton Keynes: Open University Press.

Lewis, S. and Cooper, C.L. (1999) The work–family agenda in changing contexts, *Journal of Occupational Health Psychology*, 4(4): 382–93.

Littlemore, J. (2001) The use of metaphor in university lectures and the problems that it causes for overseas students, *Teaching in Higher Education*, 6(3): 333–49.

Lodge, D. (1975) *Changing Places*. Harmondsworth: Penguin.

Lupton, D. and Barclay, L. (1997) *Constructing Fatherhood: Discourses and Experiences*. London: Sage Publications.

Mason, J. (2002) *Qualitative Researching*. London: Sage Publications.

Murray, R. (2002) *How to Write a Thesis*. Buckingham: Open University Press.

Nichol, H. and Timmins, F. (2005) Programme-related stressors among part-time undergraduate nursing students, *Journal of Advanced Nursing*, 50(1): 93.

Open University (2004a) Prospectus, *Undergraduate Certificates, Diplomas and Degrees 2005/2006*. Leicester: Artisan Press.

Open University (2004b) *Catalogue, Undergraduate Courses 2005/06*. Leicester: Artisan Press.

Pearson, A. (2003) *I Don't Know How She Does It*. London: Vintage.

Philips, E.M. and Pugh, D.S. (2005) *How to Get a PhD: A Handbook for Students and their Supervisors*. Maidenhead: Open University Press.

Puwar, N. (2004) *Space Invaders: Race, Gender and Bodies Out of Place*. Oxford: Berg.

Ramsay, K. and Letherby, G. (2006) The experience of academic non-mothers in the gendered university, *Gender, Work and Organization*, 13(1): 25–44.

Richardson, L. and Wolfe, M. (2001) *Principles and Practice of Informal Education: Learning through Life*. London: Routledge.

Richardson, P.W. (2004) Reading and writing from textbooks in higher education: a case study from Economics, *Studies in Higher Education*, 29(4): 502–21.

Sachs, J. (2002) A path model for students' attitude to writing a thesis, *Scandinavian Journal of Educational Research*, 46(1): 99–108.

Sakthivel, T. (2003) Learning and teaching in practice, *Pharmacy Education*, 3(4): 217–22.

Sargant, K. (2000) I Cyborg, in N. Greenfield (ed.) *How I Got My Postgraduate Degree Part-time*. Lancaster: Independent Studies Series.

Saunders, M., Lewis, P. and Thornhill, A. (2000) *Research Methods for Business Students*. Harlow: Financial Times/Prentice-Hall.

Talbot, C. (2003) *Studying at a Distance*. Maidenhead: Open University Press.

Tracy, E. (2006) *The Student's Guide to Exam Success*. Maidenhead: Open University Press.

Woodhams, C. and Corby, S. (2003) Defining disability in theory and practice: a critique of the British Disability Discrimination Act 1995, *Journal of Social Policy*, 32(2): 159–78.

Wright, S. and Lander, D. (2003) Collaborative group interactions of students from two ethnic backgrounds, *Higher Education Research and Development*, 22(3): 237–51.

Yum, J.C.K., Kember, D. and Siaw, I. (2005) Coping mechanisms of part-time students, *International Journal of Lifelong Education*, 24(4): 303.

Index

Locators shown in *italics* refer to case studies.

achievement, feelings of
  on study completion, 150–51, *150*
activities, social
  balancing study-social commitments,
    52–7, *54, 55, 56, 57*
advertising, course
  message limitations, 36–7, *41–2*
advice, student
  extent of facilities, 39–40
Al (case study)
  study budgeting, 31
Alex (case study)
  difficulty of formal writing, 137
  plagiarism, 105
  study time negotiation, 52
Alison (case study)
  plagiarism, 105
Annabel (case study)
  balancing home-study
    commitments, 56
answers, examination
  criteria for success, 112–14
anxiety, examination
  nature and reason, 109–12, *111*
applicability, of theoretical concepts
  as purpose of assignments, 75
assessment, examination
  nature and purpose, 109–11, *111*
assignments
  purpose, 73–6
  writing of, 76–82, *79, 82*, 118–23, *121*
attention, personal
  lack of as student, 37–8, *41–2*
attrition, course
  acknowledgement and withdrawal
    strategies, 128–33, *129–31*
  pattern and rates, 119–20
  see also suspension, study

Auger, V., 58
authorship
  crediting, 98–9
  see also plagiarism; references and
    referencing

Banks, A. (Tony), 69
bibliographies
  importance, 80, 95
  see also references and referencing
Bloom, H., 153
Bonnie (case study)
  course complaint, 148
Boyle, P., 88, 89, 91, 92, 93, 95, 138,
    140, 141
breaks, study
  reasons for, 121
  strategies for resuming study, 123–8
budgeting, study, 30–32, *31, 32*

Callow, P., 91, 134
Caroline (case study)
  Open University study, 18–19
case studies, student *see name* eg Gina;
    Paul
Cath (case study)
  joint-study, 56
Chan, S., 59
Changing Places (Lodge), 135–6
chats, online
  value as writing encouragement,
    142–3
Chekhov, A., 91, 134
Cherry, D., 68
Childhood and Youth Studies degree
    (Open University), 11–12
Chris (case study)
  joint-study, 56

Chrissie (case study)
time planning, 27
Clark, R., 138–9, 141
Collinson, D. and M., 50
Collis, S., 150
commitments, external
management planning, 26–7, 27
see also family and family life
complaints
appropriate approaches, 147–8, 148
completion, degree
personal emotions, 150–51, 150,
153–5, 154, 155
rates of, 8
completion, study
point at which achieved, 92–3
concepts, theoretical
applicability as purpose of
assignments, 75
conclusions, dissertation/thesis
importance and content, 93–4
conflicts
student-tutor conflict, 144–6
within group study, 63–7, 65, 66–7
consolidation, learning
as purpose of assignments, 74
convenience
as advantage of distance learning, 14
of university location, 24–6, 25
Cooper, C., 50
Corby, S., 68
costs, course
calculation of, 30–32, 31, 32
courses, study
characteristics, 10–13
costs and funding, 29–33, 31, 32
duration, 32–3
marketing, 36–7, 41–2
see also attrition; course; studying
credits
Open University system of, 12–13
cultures, socio-economic
difficulty for overseas students, 58–60

Dan (case study)
course negotiation, 124
deadlines
management of, 42–8, 45, 46–7, 48
see also prioritization

degrees
duration of studies, 23
rates of completion, 8
degrees, doctoral
study demands and nature, 151–3,
152
Delamont, S., 88–9, 141, 144, 146
disagreements
student-tutor conflict, 144–6
within group study, 63–7, 65, 66–7
discrimination
sexual, 68–9
dissertations and theses
prevention of writers block, 137–8
reasons for study slippage, 118–23,
121
submission, 92–3
writing of, 82–9
see also assignments
see also part and processes eg
bibliographies; goals, writing;
references and referencing; styles,
writing
distance learning
advantages and disadvantages,
13–16, 16
definition and characteristics, 10–13,
11
Dodds, A., 24
drafts, written
achievement strategies, 140–43
dropout, course
acknowledgement and strategies,
128–33, 129–31
pattern and rates, 119–20
Duke University (USA), 145–6
DuLong, J., 146
duration, course
estimation of, 32–3

editing, assignment, 80–81
Eli (case study)
difficulties of studying overseas,
61
Elizabeth (case study)
assignment planning, 79
procrastination, 46
student networks, 48
study priorities., 51

employment
    pressures from, 49–50
encouragement, study
    levels of provision, 38–40
    role in part-time situation, 20–22, *22*
    see also methods and sources eg family;
        joint study; networks, student;
        tutors/supervisors
equal opportunities
    university policies, 69–71
    see also discrimination
Erin (case study)
    study time negotiation, 52
essays
    purpose, 73–6
    writing of, 76–82, *79, 82*, 118–23,
        121
evaluation, learning
    as purpose of assignments, 74
examinations
    examiner expectations, 76
    nature and purpose, 109–11, *111*
    planning during, 112–14
    suggestions for peak outcomes,
        115–16
expectations
    examiner, 76
    student-university, 36–42, *41–2*
    university-student, 38–40, *41–2*
    see also relationships, personal;
        tutors/supervisors

family and family life
    assistance from, 47–8
    balancing study-social commitments,
        52–7, *54, 55, 56, 57*
    strain for distance learning students,
        15–16, *16*
Farley, A., 45–6, *46*, 50
feasibility
    of study topic, 84–5
feedback, assignment, 81–2, *82*
fees, course
    calculation, 30–32, *31, 32*
    considerations when self-funding,
        29–30
    see also costs, course
females
    discrimination against, 68–9

finance, course
    practical considerations, 29–33, *31,
        32*
flexibility
    as advantage of distance learning,
        14–15
flexible learning, 9–10
Flowerdew, R., 82–3, 87
'free-writing' style, 139
friendships
    assistance from, 47–8
    strain for distance learning students,
        15–16, *16*
    see also relationships, personal
funding, course
    practical considerations, 29–33, *31,
        32*

Gatrell, C., 67–8, 83, 87, 93, 99–100,
    113, 115–16, 124, 125, 151, 152–3
Giles, K., 73, 74–5, 77
Gina (case study)
    being a single status student, 57
goals, writing
    setting of, 44–5, *45*, 139–40
group study
    advantages and disadvantages,
        62–71, *65, 66–7*

Habu, T., 60
Hakim, C., 99
harassment, sexual, 146–7
Hard Labour (Gatrell), 151
Harvard system (referencing), 99
Hashim, I., 58, 59
Hedge, N., 73, 74–5, 77
Hendry, C., 45–6, *46*, 50
Hilary Swallow (case study)
    writing styles, 135–6, 141
Holtham, S., 32–3, 77, 113
home life
    assistance from, 47–8
    balancing study-social commitments,
        52–7, *54, 55, 56, 57*
    strain for distance learning students,
        15–16, *16*
Horseford, A., 21–2, 39
How to Write a Thesis (Murray), 35, 82
Hughes, B., 109

hypotheses, research
   need and importance, 87–8
   see also ideas, research

ideas, research
   generation of, 141–3
   internet as source, 84
   see also 'free writing'; goals, writing
I don't Know How She Does It (Pearson),
   135
Imogen (case study)
   feedback, 82
   student networks, 22
   study slippage, 121
'incentives'
   aid to study perseverance, 47
inclusion, university life
   difficulties for 'presence' students,
      21–2
instructions, assignment
   importance of adherence, 77
instructions, degree
   importance of adherence, 17–19,
      18–19
intellectual property
   value and protection, 102–3
   see also originality, research
interest, personal
   pre-requisite for academic writing, 87
internet
   plagiarism tool, 97
   source of topic ideas, 84
isolation, social
   countering, 40, 41–2(tab), *47*
   see also expectations, student-
      university; inclusion, university life
Ivanic, R., 138–9, 141

Jack (case study)
   balancing home-study life, 54
   feelings of loss on completion, 155
   study reasons, 7
James (case study)
   feelings of loss on completion, 154
Jan (case study)
   fee reimbursement, 32
Jane (case study)
   personal expectation management,
      41–2

plagiarism, 106–7, 107–8
Jane Smith (case study)
   study slippage, 126–7
Jasmin (case study)
   study routine, 91
Jason (case study)
   distance learning, 25
Jenna (case study)
   group study difficulties, 65
Joanna (case study)
   examination stress, 111
   experience of Open University, 11, 16
Joe (case study)
   joint study, 56
Joseph (case study)
   study completion, 150
joint study, 56, *56*

Katherine (case study)
   dropout, 129, 130–31, 132
Kember, D., 53
knowledge, demonstration of
   as purpose of assignments, 74–5

Lander, D., 59
language, English
   barrier for overseas students, 59–60
learning
   balancing study-social commitments,
      52–7, *54, 55, 56, 57*
   demands *see* examinations; writing
      up, dissertation/thesis
   resuming strategies following breaks,
      123–8
   student responsibility for managing,
      40–42, *41–2*
   trends in part-time popularity, *7–8*
   types and modes *see eg* degrees;
      distance learning; group study;
      joint study; open learning;
      'presence'
Letherby, G., 57
Lewis, S., 50
libraries, university
   extent of available services, 39
Linda (case study)
   threats to personal relations, 55
'linear writing' style, 138–9
Littlemore, J., 59

location, university
    convenience as acceptance factor,
        24–6, *25*
Lodge, D., 135–6
loneliness
    countering, 40, *41–2*
loss, feelings of
    on study completion, 153–5, *154, 155*
Luke (case study)
    course dropout, 129–31

Martin, D., 82–3
Mason, J., 83
Matt (case study)
    joint study, 56
Methods in Human Geography
    (Flowerdew), 82–3
modules, course
    characteristics, 12–13
Moss, M., 28
motivation, study
    advantages of 'presence', 20–22, *22*
    strain for distance learning students,
        15–16, *16*
    see also deadlines; prioritization;
        procrastination
Murray, R., 35, 82, 88, 89, 93, 137, 139,
    140, 141, 142

networks, students
    value and importance, 48, *48*
Nick (case study)
    part-time study, 66–7
nonconformism
    within group study, 67–8

Ohio University, 145
open learning, 9–10
Open University, 10–13, *11, 16,
    18–19*
opinions, author
    styles of referencing, 99–100
opportunities, equal
    policies, 69–71
    see also discrimination
originality, research
    need and importance, 87–8,
        101–2
Overby, L, 58

overpayment, fee, 29–30

Paul (case study)
    social isolation, 47
    balancing home-study life, 54
Pearson, A., 135
performance, examination
    suggestions for peak outcomes,
        115–16
    see also planning
PhD studies
    study demands and nature, 151–3,
        152
Philips, E., 101
plagiarism
    definition and seriousness, 96–101
    internet as medium, 97
    student vulnerability, 104–8, *105,
        106, 107–8*
    via group study, 63–4
planning
    academic writing, 77–9, *79,*
        138–43
    during examinations, 112–14
Pollock, G., 68
'presence'
    advantages and disadvantages as
        mode of study, 20–22, *22*
presentation, assignment, 79–80
*Principles and Practice of Informal
    Learning* (Richardson and Wolfe),
        114
prioratization
    study schedules, 49–52, *51, 52*
procrastination, student, 46, *46–7*
property, intellectual
    value and protection, 102–3
    see also originality, research
publicity, course
    message limitations, 36–7, *41–2*
Pugh, D., 101
Puwar, N., 68–9

questions, research
    need and importance, 87–8

Ramsay, K., 57
'recommendations', dissertation/thesis
    importance and content, 93–4

reductions, fee, 29–30
references and referencing
  importance, 80, 95
  styles of, 99–100
reimbursement, costs, 31–2, *32*
relationships, personal
  strain for distance learning students,
    15–16, *16*
  strain of 'presence' study, 21
  threat of studies, 54–5, *55*
  see also family and family life;
    friendships
requirements, degree
  importance of adherence, 17–19,
    18–19
research, work-based
  advantages and pitfalls, 85–6, *86*
Research Methods for Business Students
  (Saunders), 83
resilience
  student requirement, 37–8, *41–2*
'rewards'
  as aid to study perseverance, 47
Richardson, L., 114
routines, study
  establishment of, 90–92, *91*

Sachs, J., 119
Sakthivel, T., 60
Sanders, T., 84
Sargant, K. (case study), 129, 130–31,
  132
Saunders, M., 83
self-assurance
  student requirement, 37–8, *41–2*
Sex Work: a Risky Business (Sanders),
  84
Simenon, G., 90
slippage, study
  coping mechanisms, 123–8, *121*
  reasons for, 118–23
Smith, J. (case study)
  study slippage, 126–7
Sophie (case study)
  feelings of loss on completion, 154
sources, research
  crediting, 98–9
  see also plagiarism; references and
    referencing

Space Invaders: Bodies Out of Place
  (Puwar), 68
stress, examination
  nature and reason, 109–12, *111*
students
  case studies *see name eg* Eli; Gina
  difficulties of social inclusion, 21–2
  expectations of university, 36–42,
    41–2
  personal qualities required, 37–8,
    41–2
  student-supervisor relations, 144–6
  see also learning; relationships,
    personal; support, students
students, disabled
  advantages of distance learning,
    13–14
students, international
  study difficulties, 27–8, 58–62, *61*
students, single status
  expectations from others, 57, *57*
studying
  balancing study-social commitments,
    52–7, *54, 55, 56, 57*
  demands *see* examinations; writing,
    academic
  establishment of routines, 90–92, *91*
  resuming strategies following breaks,
    123–8
  student responsibility for managing,
    40–42, *41–2*
  trends in part-time popularity, *7–8*
  types and modes *see eg* degrees;
    distance learning; group work;
    joint study; open learning;
    'presence'
styles, writing
  barrier to academic progress, 135–8
  see also 'free writing'; 'linear writing'
subjects, study
  choice of, 83–8, *86*
submission, dissertation/thesis
  judging moment of, 92–3
supervisors/tutors
  personal assistance from, 38
  supervisor-student relations, 144–6
support, student
  levels of provision, 38–40
  role in part-time situation, 20–22, *22*

see also methods and sources eg family; joint study; networks, student; tutors/supervisors
suspension, study
    circumstances permitting, 123–4
    see also withdrawal, study
Suvorin, A., 134
Swallow, H. (case study)
    writing styles, 135–6, 141
Swallow, P., 135–6, 141

Talbot, C., 10, 38, 63, 81, 129
talks, online
    value as writing encouragement, 142–3
tasklists
    value as writing encouragement, 141–2
taster courses, 17, 28
teachers
    personal assistance from, 38
    teacher-student relations, 144–6
tensions
    student-tutor tensions, 144–6
    within group study, 63–7, *65, 66–7*
tests
    examiner expectations, 76
    nature and purpose, 109–11, *111*
    planning during, 112–14
    suggestions for peak outcomes, 115–16
theses and dissertations
    prevention of writers block, 137–8
    reasons for study slippage, 118–23, *121*
    submission, 92–3
    writing of, 82–9
    see also assignments
    see also part and processes eg bibliographies; goals, writing; references and referencing; styles, writing
time
    management in examinations, 112
time, study
    balancing study-social commitments, 52–7, *54, 55, 56, 57*
    management of, 42–8, *45, 46–7, 48, 125–8, 126–7*

planning of, 26–7, *27*
    see also breaks, study; routines, study; slippage, study; suspension, study
timeframes and timetables
    characteristics, 12–13
    planning and adherence, 32–3, 44–6, *45, 46*
topics, study
    choice of, 83–8, *86*
Turnbull, S., 67–8, 83, 93, 113, 115–16, 124, 125
tutors/supervisors
    personal assistance from, 38
    tutor-student relations, 144–6

understanding, demonstration of
    as purpose of assignments, 74–5
universities
    convenience of location, 24–6, *25*
    equal opportunities policies, 69–71
    see also name eg Duke University; Open University
    see also personnel and facilities eg libraries, university; students; tutors/supervisors

Vancouver system (referencing), 99
viewpoints, author
    styles of referencing, 99–100

websites
    plagiarism tool, 97
    source of topic ideas, 84
withdrawal, study
    acknowledgement and strategies, 128–33, *129–31*
    pattern and rates, 119–20
    see also suspension, study
Wolfe, M., 115
women
    discrimination against, 68–9
Woodhams, C., 68
work, remunerated
    pressures from, 49–50
worldwide web
    plagiarism tool, 97
    source of topic ideas, 84
Wright, S., 59

'writers block'
   prevention of, 137–8
   see also goals, writing; talks, online;
     tasklists
writing, academic
   attributes for success, 84–5, 87–8
   planning of, 77–9, *79,* 138–43
   progress difficulties, 134–8, 139–43,
     137

   styles, 138–9
writing up, dissertation/thesis,
   88–9

Your MBA With Distinction (Gatrell),
   83
Yum, J., 43

Zhiliang, Y., 58, 59